James Park is Director of Antidote, the think-tank that explores the emotional issues behind contemporary political debates and promotes the cause of emotional literacy. He is the author of two books on British cinema and of *Shrinks: The Analysts Analyzed*, a critical look at what psychotherapists get up to in their consulting rooms. He also edited *Cultural Icons*, a guide to the people who shaped the late twentieth century. He is training to become a therapist at the Centre for Attachment Based Psychoanalytic Psychotherapy.

'In this sensitive and compassionate discussion of how men's emotional hesitancies affect their intimate relationships, James Park shows us the tragic constraints and ambivalences which our sons absorb about what kind of emotions they can express.'

Susie Orbach,
psychotherapist and author of *What is Going on Here?*

'This is one of the very few books that succeeds in exploring the ways in which men are wounded by their childhood experiences without blaming their mothers. It offers an insightful argument about the role that mothers (and fathers too) play in society generally and illuminates, in a clear and accessible way, many of today's hot debates about gender, parenting and the family. James Park takes a big risk in combining his personal material with accounts of the lives of other men, but it pays off. The result is an honest and vivid account of a wide range of male experience, one that women and men at all stages of life should read.'

Professor Andrew Samuels,
Jungian Analyst and author of *The Political Psyche*

'James Park's very readable text carries you along with narrative and quotations, but does not oversimplify the essential paradoxes and awkwardnesses in the lives of boys and men as they move through the relationships they have with their mothers and lovers.'

Sebastian Kraemer, Child Psychologist

'This is a thoughtful exploration of how boys and men struggle to develop and sustain acceptable versions of male identity. The examples and case histories are sensitively presented and build into an accessible argument that succeeds in combining an insightful delivery of theory with a critical but appreciative tone.'

Paul van Heeswyk,
Consultant Child and Adolescent Psychotherapist

D1343972

Sons, Mothers
and Other Lovers

JAMES PARK

An *Abacus* Book

First published in Great Britain by Little, Brown 1995
This edition published by Abacus 1996

A CIP catalogue record for this book
is available from the British Library.

ISBN 0 349 10740 8

Typeset by Palimpsest Book Production Limited,
Polmont, Stirlingshire
Printed and bound in Great Britain by
Clays Ltd, St Ives PLC

Abacus
A Division of
Little, Brown and Company (UK)
Brettenham House
Lancaster Place
London WC2E 7EN

Acknowledgements

I am most indebted to all to those people who were willing to be interviewed by me, whose identities I promised not to reveal. I would also like to thank the following for the assistance that they offered me while I was writing this book: Cat Ledger, Clare Downs, Matthew Reisz, Françoise Delas-Reisz, Avril Wardrop, Vivienne Creevey, Deirdre Headon, Jen McClelland and Steve Hilditch. I owed many of the book's better insights to conversations with a number of therapists who kindly found time to talk with me: Jonathan Courage, Heather Formaini, Paul van Heeswyck, Susie Orbach, Andrew Samuels, Chrysoula Worrall and Ann Zachary. The book could not have been written if Lali Gostich, James Upton, Eve Upton, Susie Moberley, Guy Moberley, Rosemary McGowan, Diana Reynell, Fay Avsec, Lorna Hill, Nicky Maitlis, Vanessa Park and Mary Park had not put me in touch with mothers or sons who were willing to be interviewed. I also owe an enormous amount to my agent Julian Alexander for everything that he did to make this a book of which I could feel proud.

This book is dedicated to Ondine, who spent the months of its composition pursuing good health in Latin America, but insisted on the various drafts being sent by courier to her jungle hideaways.

There are things about men that I am completely mystified about, even though I have loved them and slept with them all my life.

Germaine Greer

Contents

Introduction

Men will do the strangest things in order to avoid getting close to other people. Some develop a rash whenever any woman shares their bed, so that those girlfriends who are invited in for sex end up sleeping on the sofa. Some walk coatless into snowstorms as a way of cutting short a matrimonial tiff about who should be invited to a dinner party. Others respond to the news that a partner is going into hospital for a major operation by putting up shelves in the kitchen or buying her a new car, rather than asking how she might be feeling. There are men too who volunteer to work overtime so that they do not have to talk with their children, and others who follow a bout of lovemaking by lighting a cigarette, getting out of bed and going downstairs to watch television.

There seems to be no obvious reason why men should be so bad at coping with the demands that relationships place upon them. They grow up in the same families as girls do, go to the same schools, listen to the same music and watch the same soaps on TV. And yet they do not seem to develop the same ability for relating to other people, or for knowing what it is they feel.

Even when in later life some men come to acknowledge that the cultivation of a meaningful marriage or a wide circle of friends might be more desirable than acquiring an expensive car, a large office and a beer belly, they mostly find it impossible to do much about changing themselves. They may huff and puff their way through ante-natal classes, push prams around public parks and gather the family shopping from supermarket shelves – things that few of their fathers and none of their grandfathers would have contemplated doing – but this does not necessarily improve their ability to do the work that relationships require.

Men have these problems with intimacy for much the same reason that they cannot speak Sanskrit, walk on their hands, or behead a chicken: they never learned how to do it. They pick up in their mothers' arms the lesson that it is better to keep some distance between themselves and others; for while the experience of her embrace brings great pleasure, it also arouses strange terrors.

When a boy is a little babe who can do nothing for himself, mother will pick him up, put him down, stroke him, pat him, drop him, cuddle him and decide when he will be fed or cleaned. The feelings of warmth and contentment she stirs up make him want to enjoy with her an ever-closer intimacy. But alongside this 'good' mother, there is the 'bad', the one who disciplines him and constrains him, the mother whose power seems sometimes set to crush him. She can make him feel fearful, inadequate and powerless. He learns to hate her and wants to destroy her before, that is, she sets about destroying him.

Mother becomes more fearful to a boy as he learns that she is of another sex, and comes to recognise how much less, under traditional parenting arrangements, father is engaged in his care. Whereas a sister can look forward to the time when she will wield over another the power now turned against her, the boy experiences himself as being essentially on his own, without any clear sense of what his future might be. Because the face he sees in front of him is mostly female, and because he does not have sufficient access to a male who can convince him that he too will one day be in control, he experiences himself as being utterly defenceless, dangerously subject to the domination of another.

He senses that his mother looks upon him as a representative of another gender, and brings to their relationship a complex set of feelings that derive from her experience of other men. When she conveys to him her love, neediness or anxiety, the slant is different from that communicated to any daughter: she asks him to make things right for her in his capacity as a male. And there is often nobody around who is committed to showing him how to deal with that sort of pressure.

Children of both sexes mature by wresting from their parents the power to do for themselves what was once done for them, even while they still cling close to mother for emotional support. As the boy struggles to bring his longing for love and his need for independence into some sort of balance, he begins to feel that something is being asked of him which he cannot deliver – that he is inadequate, weak and therefore in danger. Moving anxiously away from mother, he learns to value autonomy over togetherness. He wants to control situations because he dare not surrender to the pleasures available from connection.

The experience of being truly close to someone else, whether man or woman, puts him at risk of experiencing again the same bewildering emotions that he knew in infancy. He may come to dominate boardrooms, control companies, command budgets of millions and make the key decisions about family life, but it will not necessarily help if he still feels just as weak, susceptible and terrified of coming close to another as he did when his life was completely controlled by mother. Given those early experiences, he can never enjoy intimacy without feeling to some degree in peril, even though the source of that fear is hidden deep in his psyche.

He may feel driven to drink half a bottle of whisky if he hears his wife laughing with her friends in the lounge, being quite convinced that the object of their hilarity can only be himself. He may hide behind a newspaper in the morning so as to fend off any demands from his wife or children. And he may be inspired by his belief that his wife now considers him an inadequate performer in bed to embark upon a superficial fling and thoughtlessly put at risk his main relationship. He will not be able to talk coherently about any of these reactions – until, that is, he comes to understand how they relate to his early experiences with mother.

There is a long history of mothers being blamed for all the inadequacies of men. They are told that if they had been more attentive, less distant or less smothering, their boys would have developed much more confidence in their masculinity and more facility in their relationships. What such critics never ask of any particular mother is why she might behave in this way towards her son, or what the other parent was doing at the time. Thus Robert Bly, the pugnacious guru of the men's movement, criticises mothers for their 'possessiveness' in his book, *Iron John*, which is otherwise quite perceptive about how men are affected by the emotional absence of their fathers. So powerful is Bly's nostalgia for the lifestyles of those 'primitive' tribes where boys spend their early years in the exclusive care of women before being dragged screaming into the masculine world that he is incapable of following his own logic and encouraging men to become involved, nurturing fathers throughout the whole period when their children are growing up. Their only function, it seems, is to wrench boys away from the feminine world.

Given the criticism that mothers have endured, it did not surprise me that so many women responded with mild paranoia when they learned about this book, being apparently unable to conceive of my project as anything other than an attack upon them. 'You are evil', one of them said to me. I argue, though, that it is fathers, not mothers, who are mostly responsible for the emotional problems that afflict so many men. Having only one parent upon whom he can really lean, a boy becomes so intensely caught up in his relationship with her that he cannot but respond defensively to the pressures placed upon him. What he needs is someone else to help him deal with the terror which she can provoke so that he can gain a glimpse of how she really is – most likely a woman trying to do the best she can in difficult circumstances. Only the presence of an attentive father, or a father-substitute, willing to expose his strengths and weaknesses, someone who will listen to him and talk with him, can neutralise the boy's anxieties about intimacy with her.

The assertion that boys (and girls) need fathers might sound like some back-to-basics call for the return of old, two-parent, family values. It is no such thing. Men have to provide a considerably better service to their own children than they themselves received from their fathers, and to be as engaged with their children as mothers have traditionally been. Spending a few more hours in every week with the kids is as inadequate a response to their needs as a few minutes hoovering is to the call for men to do more housework.

All boys confront the same problem: how to feel strong in the presence of an all-powerful and demanding mother. But the solutions they adopt can take many forms, depending on the particular dynamic of the relationships they have with their parents and others. The attitudes developed in childhood tend, though, to shape a man's later attitudes to women; only when he can learn – as many never do – that women do not have the powers which his infantile mind ascribed to them, will it be possible for him to break free and transform himself.

Not all men succeed in evolving strategies that will give them the upper hand. The Lovelorn is so crippled by the sense that his mother did not much care for him, that he is unable to believe in the love offered by anyone else. The Lover Son, having been adopted by his mother as a surrogate husband, never develops the courage to break away from under her skirt and form a relationship to anyone else. The Idolater was so impressed by his mother's strength, and saw so little evidence of a father's countervailing force, that he ends up spending his life in thrall to powerful women.

There are other men, though, who are more successful at building up defensive structures. The Wild Man, for example, learns to give no quarter in his striving for dominance and control. He is driven, obsessive, inclined to grandiosity and megalomania, and the sheer force of his personality carries others in his wake. The Chauvinist develops an exclusive definition of masculinity as part of a strategy to ensure that a woman will always be available to take care of his needs. By never learning to cook, sew or clean, he provides himself with a ready pretext for calling upon a woman's aid. The Trad Man too relies upon a clear definition of the gender divide, but he is more willing than the Chauvinist to consider occasionally crossing the line. The Seducer deals with his fear of the emotions which women can evoke by never letting himself get too close. He declares that he adores women, even as his callous indifference to their feelings shows that he fears and hates them.

This book interweaves accounts of these seven male types with chapters that look more generally at the process by which a boy becomes a man. I show how a mother's experience of men, and her feelings about masculinity, shape the attitudes she takes to her sons. I then examine how the young boy depends upon his mother's love to give him the inner strength that he needs if he is to move away from her and establish his autonomy.

Subsequent chapters show how a boy acquires his sense of what it means to be a male, and how he deals with the realisation that his mother has important relationships with people other than himself. There is then an exploration of how the adolescent boy builds up his confidence to the point where he is able to leave his mother and establish a relationship to someone else. After attempting to fathom the source of sexual desire, and how it is shaped by a man's experience of his mother, I describe the emotional pressures that boys experience from their mothers because they are male, especially where these force them to close off their emotions. Following a chapter on male violence against women, I conclude by looking at the various proposals which have been made for reducing a boy's sense that his mother is a dangerous, controlling and constricting force, and at some possible solutions to the problems between men and women.

The book is based on 150 interviews I carried out over two years, in which I heard from their own mouths or from those of their mothers (and often from both) about how a group of men experienced the women in their lives. In my search to uncover all the ways in which boys respond to their mothers' influence, I spoke with at least one judge, builder, accountant, company director, farmer, designer, dustman, furniture remover, painter, sculptor, civil servant, engineer, financier, gentleman of leisure, actor and drag artist. I also talked to various psychotherapists and counsellors who offered me further help in understanding how men's attitudes to women are shaped by the relationships they have with their mothers.

CHAPTER ONE

Mothers of Men

'A mother melts when she sees her son,' author Rachel Billington has written. 'He is amazing, extraordinary, head-burning.' She goes on to suggest that such feelings have a profound influence on the way mothers treat their boys: 'We spoil our sons, not because we think they deserve it, but because they are a kind of miracle which befogs our usual calm good sense.'[1] While some mothers claim that they treat all their children, whether male or female, in exactly the same way, most – although less rhapsodic on the subject than Billington – would agree that a son stirs up feelings quite different from those experienced upon the arrival of a girl.

There are women who really do want only that their child be born healthy. Others can put forward good reasons for preferring girls: who are, for one thing, less likely to bombard their mothers with endless variants on the themes of Action Man, He-Man and macho man. But when confronted by researchers walking around maternity wards with clipboards in their hands, most mothers who feel strongly on the subject say they would rather have a son. My own mother clearly once belonged in this category. 'I was determined,' she says of the period before my birth, 'to have a boy. That made everyone angry with me, but it was the most wonderful thing in the world, as magic as I thought it was going to be.'

It is not so difficult to understand why a woman might feel a special rush of excitement at the arrival of a baby boy. He may have no facial hair nor any strength in his muscles, and the sounds he utters will usually be very squeaky, but his penis indicates that he will become a man. As such, he offers his mother the opportunity to experience, albeit at second-hand, what it is to grow up male: a radically new experience that no daughter can provide. 'I wanted to give birth, at twenty-five, to my unborn self,' wrote American poet and feminist Adrienne Rich of her longing for a son, 'the self that our father-centered family had suppressed in me, someone independent, actively willing, original.'[2]

The feelings that a mother has towards her boy will be shaped by her previous experiences of men, and they are not likely to be as wholly positive and uncomplicated as Billington suggests. She may want a son to help her relive a blissful experience of father, or to bestow upon her the sort of love she feels no man has ever given her before, or just to give her a sense of how it feels to possess a male body. She may hope to create a man more adequate and satisfactory than any she experienced in her life before. She may attempt to find through her male child the confidence, purposefulness and ambition that she cannot quite summon up in herself. Or she may want to inflict upon him all the resentment that she feels about not having been brought up a boy, and not having received the privileges that were allocated to brothers.

The ambivalence which a mother feels about masculinity can be extremely oppressive to her son. She may try to knock out of him male traits of which she does not approve. She may seek to insulate him from other men so that he will not be tainted by their values. She may hold him close so that she can turn him into her toy-boy, her lover-boy, her mama's boy, or whatever else she fancies. And as he proves increasingly recalcitrant to her influence, stubbornly asserting his male identity as something separate from hers, she may let him know that the pleasure which his gender once gave her has dissipated; she no longer wants anything more to do with a man like him. The fact that she is often barely conscious of such feelings and desires can render their impact all the more powerful.

I believe that mothers can be divided into three different types. The Celebratory Mother has strong views about what a man should be, and while she is keen to celebrate her son's maleness, she will do so only as long as it conforms to those ideas. The Ambivalent Mother has more mixed feelings about men. She may accept her husband or partner pretty much as he is, but nevertheless convey quite strongly to her son the desire that he be somewhat different. The third type is the Demanding Mother, who envies her son his masculinity, revels in the power over a male that her son's arrival gives her and sometimes uses his birth to free herself from all other relationships to men.

Celebratory Mothers

The Celebratory Mother tends to have an almost mystical view of what it means to be a man. Having usually experienced her father as a warm and loving presence, she learned to idolise him and to revel in her capacity to attract his regard. Enjoying the recognition that is given to her as a woman, and with no particular reason to envy men whatever advantages they have, she is not interested in usurping males from their positions of authority. Having no doubt that there is a distinct line separating men from women, she tends to feel largely happy with the consequences, and to look for partners who, by their difference from her, will confirm her identity as a woman.

Rebecca, for example, has a husband who describes her as the antithesis of himself: a 'sort of whirlwind, zany and unpredictable', who displays 'luscious beauty', 'intelligence' and 'delightful ebullience'. With his bald head, angular features and long neck, he is a little dry, emotionally distant, witty, an intellectual – clearly very different from the creative and volatile Rebecca. As we talked, he made several jokes about the moodiness of his wife and daughters. 'It just seems to go with the female territory, as far as I can make out,' he says.

When Rebecca talks somewhat enigmatically about 'the extraordinary purity' that she has noticed in young boys and the 'bravery' of adolescents as they struggle towards manhood, it is to emphasise the gap that she sees between male and female. She says of her son, who is now in his mid-thirties, that he was 'male at birth', which is not some banal reference to his genitalia but a description of certain qualities which, she says, he displayed from his earliest days. Even as a wee baby, she suggests, he was an emotional rock upon which she could weep: he was only thirteen months old when Rebecca turned to him for consolation following the death of her grandfather. 'I remember,' she says, 'holding on to him, this podgy little form with his nappies. He seemed to me very strong.'

I expressed to Rebecca my scepticism about whether it was really possible to assert that her son embodied such strength. Had she not imagined it to be there because she felt the need of it? But Rebecca's belief in male fortitude, even when the male concerned is still wearing nappies, would not yield to my logic. For Rebecca, men are strong through and through, and no displays of weakness or dependency on their part will convince her otherwise.

Why should she feel so strongly on this point? Her attitude seems to have evolved during three early years that she spent alone with her father (and an occasional nurse or nanny) following the death of her mother. Her memories of this time are strong. She recalls the feel of her father's tweeds against her soft skin, and his clumsiness as he wrapped a blanket around her and put her down in the cot 'like a chrysalis'. Remembering fondly the different smells that her father brought into the house, the roughness of his beard and jacket, the strength he displayed when he lifted her into his arms, the longing that his absences from the house generated, Rebecca came to associate maleness with loving strength, and this has caused her to relish the company of men ever since.

At the age of seven, when her father married again, Rebecca lost this exclusive relationship to her father. Poorly informed about the consequences of this decision, she tried to climb into the car that was taking her father and stepmother away from the wedding party. 'I had no idea,' she says, 'that from now on, I would not be going with my father wherever he went.' Despite her initial unhappiness about this change, she came eventually to accept that, being lonely, her father had to marry someone, and that it was incumbent upon her to search for another man who would be hers alone. She went on to seek from her husband – as from her son – an opportunity to renew the sense of intimacy with a man that she had lost on her father's wedding day.

The Celebratory Mother wants sons not because she thinks they are better than daughters, but because their distinctness gives her pleasure. She has no resentment of men, because she does not really feel that they have any greater opportunities in life. She thinks of herself as a winner in the sex war, someone who has turned her position as a woman to advantage. Susannah, for example, holds down a high-powered job, while managing with help from her mother and sister to look after two sons. She not only manages to 'have it all' but enjoys herself enormously at the same time. Far from draining her, this achievement thrills her.

I had been sitting for only a few minutes in the atrium of the offices where Susannah works when she appeared on the third-floor balcony and summoned me up the spiral staircase to her office. Ushered inside, I listened in while childcare arrangements were discussed over the phone with her sister, and she spoke to a female colleague about tactics for a marketing meeting to be held the next morning. I then followed as she led me through a series of security doors to the company canteen.

Generally, when mothers of boys talk about having wanted sons, one wonders whether they might not be trying to make the best of what they have been landed with. But Susannah left me in no doubt about the strength of her longing for male children. Adopting a conspiratorial tone, she confided to me that she had never talked about this subject before, even with her husband, as she quickly dismissed my question about whether the pleasure she took in her boys reflected any sort of unhappiness about her own position as a woman. 'I really would not like to be a man,' she said, remarking that she had always enjoyed the attention she received as a girl from her warm-hearted father, and as a woman from her husband. 'I do definitely like men,' she said, 'because of everything they provide that women do not.' This enigmatic remark turned out to be highly significant.

Susannah has been fortunate to find her way into working environments where being female seemed to help more than it hindered, and to enjoy circumstances which gave her a real choice between career, motherhood or a combination of the two. But did she not feel just a little resentful about the fact that her husband had never considered working part-time in order to help out with the children as she had done? 'Is it a sacrifice?' she riposted. 'I had a fantastic time for two years, scaling down my work commitments and being at home.' Whereas he would have been harshly criticised by both parents and peers for taking such a step, she was heaped with plaudits 'for being a working woman *and* managing a family'.

Susannah's husband is, in fact, as involved a father as his corporate responsibilities allow him to be. He leaves the house at 6.00 a.m. so that he can return home in time to prepare the children's supper, give them a bath, read a story and put them to bed. But Susannah holds on determinedly to her status as the primary parent by taking a day off in every week to be with the children, and by handling a much larger proportion of the childcare responsibilities. She treasures the uniqueness of her role within the family, in part because it reinforces her sense of feminine identity.

This greater commitment to parenting not only reflects her views about the difference between men and women, it influences the attitude that she adopts to her pre-school boys. Even though she experienced the time that she took out from her career as 'absolutely blissful', she does not anticipate that her boys might do the same. The expectations she has for them are, in consequence, 'slightly different' from those she would have of any daughters. 'I should not be saying this,' she remarks, resuming her conspiratorial tone, 'but if I am really honest, I do expect them to be in society's terms more successful.' She reports with pride that her second son is 'pushy', suggests that her elder boy is 'just as strong in a different way', and then asks quizzically 'Who is the natural leader?' almost as if she believed that it was a man's function to lead and a woman's to follow.

Why, though, is it so important for Susannah to see her boys behaving in a 'male' way? Perhaps because the distinctness of their masculinity, their difference from her, gives the love they offer her a special charge. 'I like living in a little male world,' Susannah says. The pleasure lies in the admiration she receives from her husband, her two sons and her father. She describes her elder son's good behaviour when an infant as 'a form of praise' and refers several times to the 'massive approval' that she feels coming from both her boys. 'They have always done,' she says, 'a really good job of making me feel totally relaxed and happy about what I am doing.' And although Susannah does not say exactly what it is that she expects from her husband, she offers a clue by wistfully anticipating the time when her sons will find a woman other than her whom they can 'deify'. Clearly, for Susannah, what men provide that women cannot is worship of her person.

The pleasure that a Celebratory Mother finds in difference makes her willing to excuse a son's noisiness, aggression and obtuseness as indications of a healthy boyishness. Convinced of the need for a firm demarcation between the sexes, she never encourages her boy to question prevailing ideas of what it means to be male or female. If her sons accept their mother's concept of masculinity, they are likely to become Trad Men (Chapter Fourteen) or Chauvinists (Chapter Nine), the two types of men most strongly resistant to the notion of equality between the sexes.

Ambivalent Mothers

Most women have had much less satisfactory experiences of father (and of other men) than Celebratory Mothers. Dad may not have shown them much affection. He may have been weak and in need of their protection, or sullen and depressed. His absence from the home and general inability to lovingly support them in the struggles of their early lives may have aroused their resentment. They may now find themselves married to men who are irritatingly dependent, emotionally inadequate or unsatisfactory in some other way.

The Ambivalent Mother believes in the possibility of a man being a good lover, friend or husband, but she repeatedly finds that reality does not match up. Successive disappointments work to ensure that she ends up with an attitude to men that is simultaneously admiring and streaked with disdain. Since only her son can revive her hope of realising the dream, she sets out to try and ensure that he will turn out more satisfactory than most of the men she has known.

Lesley is as enthusiastic as any Celebratory Mother about sexual difference. She feels that women are wrong to try and be like men, and she hopes that chivalry will never die: she is pleased when men bring her flowers and open the door for her as she passes down the corridor. But her attitude to men is also coloured by resentment and anger. She feels that her father and her husband both tried to hold her back, forcing her to fight hard for recognition as a working woman. Like many others, she could regale anyone who would listen with a long litany of complaints about men.

In her youth, Lesley's view of men was highly romanticised, but she has come to respect men less and less as they have forced upon her awareness of their emotional frailties. It was during a second pregnancy, when her mother was dying of cancer, that she first realised to what extent her father, the model of manhood upon which she had always gazed with admiration, was in fact an emotional cripple. Instead of supporting his wife through her final illness and helping her to accept that the end was near, he ran off with another woman. Lesley observed with distress that he would arrive at the hospital, displaying his new lover on his arm, and then talk with all the *other* patients in the ward. He would dismiss his daughters' disapproving glances with an insensitive remark and refused to acknowledge that his behaviour might be hurting the woman with whom he had lived for 30 years. Seeing him was unbearable after that, and Lesley cut him out of her life until shortly before he died.

This, though, was the man whom she had admired, and upon whom she had depended for support over 25 years. The terror induced by her discovery of his fragility was all the greater because Lesley was now married to a man with very similar traits. She did not know whether he could still be relied upon, this husband who not only expected complete attention from her when he was at home, but clearly needed it; for he did not know how to boil an egg, iron a shirt or sew on a button. (His chauvinism is explored more fully in Chapter Nine.) He seemed to consider too that his responsibilities to his children began and ended with writing out a cheque for the school fees.

Lesley set out to inculcate a different set of values in her boys, but the messages she conveyed were somewhat confused. She tried to encourage them not to bottle up their feelings, but shrugged her shoulders when they stopped telling her things: she blamed this development on their school. She made sure they knew something about cooking and sewing, but she still taught them to look for women who would perform these functions for them. 'I find it difficult,' she says, 'not having been brought up with the equality thing.' Her recognition of the benefits that would flow from greater equality between the sexes is tempered by the pleasure she still takes from her husband's continued dependence.

Unlike Lesley, Sophie still worships her father, remembering him as someone who was always proud of her, willing to offer a plentiful supply of love, encouragement and admiration, and his memory heightens her sense of disillusion with men; for the man she married at sixteen, when she was pregnant with the first of her two sons, was made from a very different mould. Apparently incapable of rising to the challenges of family life, he seemed to be quite overwhelmed by the hubbub that his children created. When Sophie thought that he should talk to his children and find out what they were feeling, he flogged them instead. Nor did he show them much of an example in other ways. He seemed to take little pleasure in his work and revealed no passion for anything else apart from tennis. Sophie gave me the impression that only her husband's qualities as a lover had kept the two of them together for almost thirty years (and they were to separate while I was writing the final draft of this book).

Sophie found her husband's behaviour towards their children all the more bewildering because it contrasted so radically with her own feelings. She was so ecstatic when her first child turned out to be a boy that she simply could not grasp the extent to which her husband would be unable to share this enthusiasm. 'I was over the moon,' she recalls. 'I couldn't believe it. I was so excited that I had to keep looking at his willy to make sure he had one.' Could he not see what a wonderful being they had created together? Clearly he could not. Increasingly, the enthusiasm that Sophie felt for her sons was coloured by a desire to have in the house a male presence more satisfactory than that provided by her husband.

Sophie's sons found themselves caught up in a conflict between their mother's image of men and their father's performance as a man, and early on came to recognise how far their mother would go to ensure that her own outlook would prevail. Whenever her husband suggested that they might dress differently or work harder at school, she told him to leave them alone. She encouraged him to take jobs abroad, so that she could have the boys to herself, and teach them that it was not necessary to excel in sport, as their father had done, or to aim for a life in the corporate fast lane. Instead, she wanted them to emulate their grandfather: to paint, take photographs, make pots and be happy. To a large extent, she has succeeded. 'They are creative,' she says, 'like I am.'

The Ambivalent Mother is the most likely agent of change in men. She does not hide from her sons their father's failings, nor does she try to impose upon them an idealised vision of masculinity. She enjoys aspects of their maleness, but also suggests that there are other possibilities than the ones they see around them. By giving out a message that is bound to confuse, and by attempting to manipulate her sons' responses, she encourages them to ask questions about what it is to be male, and to sense the possibility that things might be different from the way they are in the family home. When the son of an Ambivalent Mother experiences her confusion as making it impossible for her truly to care for him, he will end up in the ranks of the Lovelorn (Chapter Five): if he is more impressed by her ability to wield power over men, he may become an Idolater (Chapter Eleven).

Demanding Mothers

Some women grow up with fathers who drink away the family budget, make no attempt to hide their violent natures, rule the house with more terror than love, or simply go, leaving only their sour memory to be cursed and reviled by adult family members. Others grow up with the sort of men who find playing with their train set more enjoyable than talking with their children, or who become the butt of endless matrimonial recriminations for failing to increase their salaries in line with the expanding needs of their families. These consistently useless fathers will tend to foster in their daughters a view of masculinity that is largely negative, and will encourage them to become Demanding Mothers.

Women coming from such households will grow up without the image of a strong, self-confident man to draw upon in building their sense of self-worth. And they will never have witnessed or experienced a satisfactory relationship with a man to give them confidence in building their own adult bonds. The idea that it might be possible to find a good man is not a hope – as it is with the Ambivalent Mother – it is a fantasy. 'My experience with men,' remarked one mother to whom I spoke, 'is that they are a bit of a drain.' In her dreams, though, she imagines being married to a 'large Italian man like Pavarotti' who would say 'Come with me, I will take care of all your problems.' 'It would be wonderful,' she adds, 'to meet a man who would let me turn into a lump of jelly.'

These daughters may have a strong sense of what their father did not give them, but they will not have any real confidence in the possibility of their finding a man who could make them feel loved, cherished and generally good about themselves. By usually hitching themselves to men who are as hopeless as their fathers, they confirm this pessimistic analysis, and draw closer to concluding that the only way to find a man deserving of their love is to rear a son.

The Demanding Mother will often push the child's father into the background, or discard him completely, once he has fulfilled his inseminatory function, and he tends anyway to be the sort who has little urge to hang around. Once he is out of the way, the mother can enjoy more fully both the joys of her maternal femininity, and the opportunities available to experience masculinity through her son. I spoke to one mother who had told her husband that if he came home before 9.30 in the evening she would completely ignore him: that was time she wanted alone with her boy. He, instead of fighting this edict, welcomed the freedom that it gave him.

Such a mother clings to a baby boy as her surrogate husband and her masculine self. She has problems envisaging separation from him, because he is the only satisfactory male that she has ever known, her last chance for complete intimacy with a man. And yet she cannot fully enjoy his masculinity, the fact that he will become a man like other men, because that will mean his becoming a man who has put his mother behind him. She wants a man to stand beside her and support her, but he must not become too much like other men – the useless kind like her father or her husband, the sort who leaves or hits or neglects. As a result, she may come to resent the signs of boyishness in him; his noise, his obsession with football, his need to have the latest macho toy, his desire to fight, the misogynistic expressions that come so easily to his tongue, because they threaten her with eventual separation from him.

The son of such a woman cannot follow wherever nature and circumstances take him, because his mother has impressed upon him her need of his support. He cannot freely form relationships with others, because his mother is too fearful of losing him. 'I wanted my son for myself,' one mother said to psychoanalyst Estela Welldon, 'alone without any competition. I created an idyllic relationship with my son to the point that I didn't need any other man in my life.'[3] And when he began to rebel and push her away, she hardly knew what to do with her anger.

'I was obsessed with my baby,' says Sheila of the months after her first child James was born. Her experience with men had been of a father who lacked ambition, self-confidence or any ability to assert himself against a domineering wife, and a husband who was handsome and kind but inclined to direct his jealousies into violence or adultery. When her son was three, she threw her husband out, declaring that she would have nothing to do with any male except the 'man' who had sprung from her loins. She wanted a son who would love her, admire her and be proud of her, and for thirteen years she had him. James was affectionate, happy to kiss her, hold her hand and snuggle up on the sofa. 'That was all I really wanted,' Sheila says, 'somebody to think I was great.'

Knowing that it was not right to demand so much from her son, Sheila looked for another man, and found someone who seemed at first to be the perfect father for her children, until it emerged that he was a drug addict with violent tendencies. Instead of needing James less, Sheila called upon him more, asking him to defend her against his stepfather's aggression. 'Why do you shout at mummy?' the nine-year-old would ask, bringing waves of anger and recrimination down upon himself. And when that boyfriend had been expelled, it was perhaps because James felt such enormous pressure upon him, and did not know how to exclude himself from the flood of anti-male rhetoric that spewed forth from his mother's mouth, that he started to resent her, and pine for his long-absent father. If only Dad had stayed around, James said to himself, everything would have been okay.

James became increasingly rude to his mother. 'Who do you think you are talking to?' she asked on one occasion when his words were particularly cutting.

'And who do you think *you* are talking to?' he replied in a superior tone that seriously irritated his mother. She grabbed him, put her hands around his neck and shook him.

'I give you my time, my love, my money, my thoughts. I give up everything to make you a happy boy, and still you are not satisfied.'

At this point, James burst into tears and said, 'But you cannot give me a daddy who loves me.'

Sheila looked down at her son, saw the muscles in his neck red with blood where she had pressed with her nails and started to cry. He cuddled up to her then. 'You didn't mean it, Mummy,' he said.

The more powerful a mother's need for love, attention and physical affection from her son, the more difficult he will find it to work out his own desires and feelings. Some eighteen years after the scene described above, James is still angry with his mother. He tells her off for talking too loudly in restaurants, driving badly and not knowing how to handle her life 'properly'. He clearly wants to hurt her and to give off the impression that he does not mind what happens to her. 'All I have done is put nice into him,' Sheila complains, 'and I don't get anything nice back. I feel resentful about that. He doesn't care for me. He doesn't love me as he should.' Sheila feels that she has been short-changed on the rewards of motherhood, that she deserves better than the criticism and rebuke that her son directs at her. 'I need his support, I need his love, I need him to look after me like a man,' she says.

But James is right to be angry, to feel that his mother asked too much when she called upon him to fill the gap left by the departure of his father and then his stepfather: in fact, to make up for all the men in her life. And yet there are mothers who ask still more, mothers who continuously express their bitterness with men to their sons, mothers who initiate their sons sexually, persuading themselves that this is the natural outcome of the intimacy between them, refusing to acknowledge that they might be doing harm to their children, then recoiling in horror when their sons turn angrily against them. These Demanding Mothers trap their sons in an emotional cocoon from which they have removed all possibility of escape when they cut off relations with father. Their boys may grow up to be Seducers (Chapter Sixteen) or Lover Sons (Chapter Seven), but they will never throw off the sense that women want to smother them.

All mothers play a considerable role in shaping their sons' expectations of women and relationships. Insofar as a boy takes on all the angry, resentful, jealous and bitter feelings that his mother has about men, influence can be depicted as being extremely negative. If he absorbs the full impact of her feelings about him and learns to see himself through her eyes, he may often become confused, distressed, panicky. But the ensuing problems cannot sensibly be confronted by telling mothers that they should feel differently about men, and about their sons. If their fathers are brutes or their husbands cads, that cannot but influence a woman's feelings about her boys.

What the boy needs is a father's help in dealing with the emotional pressures that come from his mother. He needs to learn that there are other views of masculinity than those which she propounds, and that what she says to him has more to do with her own past experiences than with him. If he is to break away from her emotional control and start following his own path, he needs to learn that he will not lose her love simply because he refuses to respond to every challenge that she lays down for him.

CHAPTER TWO

Power With Security

Archie was sipping his pre-lunch whisky when he became aware that his grand-daughter sat across the room, holding his great-grandson to her breast. 'How distressing,' he ruminated, 'to think that all men start out so dependent upon a woman.'

Why should Archie react so negatively to the sight of a boy in a woman's arms, totally reliant upon her for food, warmth and security? Why should he apparently be reluctant to acknowledge that he might have enjoyed being together with his own mother? It was she, after all, who made possible his development and growth, by keeping him warm and comfortable, cleaning him, feeding him, stimulating him with her voice, her gestures, her caresses; offering up food and relief, comfort and joy, care and love.

For a mother, the early months of her child's life can be a uniquely special time. However angry, demanding and ungrateful her son may be, she can feel pleasure at finding herself at the centre of a young child's life: feeding him, stroking him and being recognised by him. I remember how often through my childhood, my mother would recall our early days together, when I lay in my pram and gurgled up at her, apparently always happy to see her. 'I would still love him to be a little baby in my arms,' Yvonne says of her thirteen-year-old son. 'It is the most generous, perfect love in a way. Nobody wants anything more than what they are getting. You have the feeling that you are their world. It makes you feel so whole.'

The extent of the boy's neediness and the mother's pre-paredness to respond creates a relationship within which both parties can hope to find satisfaction. Although enormously much stronger and more capable than him, she does not use her power *against* him, rather she gives it *to* him. Because she responds to his needs and demands, he imagines that he controls her, that she is there to service him. He can do what he wants with her. She provides the warm ground to his life.

Yet a mother's attention cannot be entirely satisfactory. There will be gaps in the service that she provides, periods when the infant boy finds that he has no power to call her. It would be impossible, as it would be undesirable, for a mother to satisfy all her child's needs. He has to learn that she will not come whenever he calls, that she will not always know when he is hungry, cold or wet. There will be hours that he spends feeling restless, frustrated, and impatient, crying alone in a room at night. Gradually he comes to realise that he must acquire resources of his own, to break his dependency upon mother and to become someone quite other.

The baby's desire to learn about, and act upon, the world, leads him away from mother. The joy of togetherness is accompanied from the start by the urge to be apart. 'Babies themselves desire to grow and separate from mother,' says psychotherapist Andrew Samuels, 'as well as to rest in oceanic bliss.'[1] From the age of six weeks or thereabouts, babies start actively to explore the world around them, touching their toes and hands, pummelling their mothers' breasts. Steadily, their field of vision broadens. They fling objects off their high table and devise ways of getting around a room. This learning process joins up with the discovery that mother is not completely there for them and brings awareness of her separateness.

Even as the boy experiments with his own capacities, he needs to feel that she is watching over him, providing him with a guarantee of security, some sort of assurance that he is not alone. The physical contact that children have with their mothers is an important source of reassurance. If this woman who is older and bigger than they are will let them cling and attack, then they know that they are probably safe. Many men recalled to me the pleasure of climbing into bed with mother. 'We used,' says Peter, 'to get a great deal of comfort from that. They were some of the happiest times.' 'When my father got up in the morning,' Ted recalls, 'I would go and get into the bed. It was a very physical, close thing. I would race through and dive into this great, warm cavity where my father had been, and lie beside my mother. It was wonderful actually, physical rapture.'

Everything he does is made possible by her presence in the background, her readiness to attend upon him when he calls. She looms above as he takes his first steps; she waits at the bottom as he slips down a slide; she follows behind as he learns to ride his tricycle. He cannot do these things unless he knows that she is there. When Eric went into hospital for an operation at the age of three and his mother left him, he bawled his eyes out 'not because I was frightened, not because the nurses weren't nice, not because I was worried about anything, but simply because of the *fact* that mother was leaving.' But all the time the boy is moving forward, feeling his way towards the day when he can break away from this person who makes him feel safe.

Her love for him and the security that she provides gives him self-worth and a sense of his capacity. 'The child must feel,' write Luise Eichenbaum and Susie Orbach, 'that its mother will not disappear; that she will be there as the anchor, the safety net of love and encouragement. With this security the child can expand its world and come to feel the world is a safe place.'[2] The mother must love him in order to free him. She creates a relationship whose purpose is to make her boy capable of moving away to form relationships with other people. The more she truly loves him, the easier he will find it to leave her. His knowledge that she cares is something that he takes with him, feeding his confidence that others will do the same.

So important to the boy is the notion of mother being there that the prospect of her disappearance arouses absolute terror. Any disturbance in the normal routine can stir his sense of insecurity. Gina remembers an afternoon when her son was six and he came rushing into the house to announce that he was dying. 'Don't be silly,' she said. He insisted that he was telling the truth. 'His eyes were like saucers,' she recalls, 'and his heart was pumping. He was trying to make me understand that he was dying. "Feel my heart," he said, "it is banging."' Gina calmed him down and did not think much more about the incident until the headmaster rang from his school later that week to ask if anyone in the family had passed away. The educational psychologist to whom he was taken concluded that Gina's son felt concern about the possibility that, since a younger brother was now at school, his mother, feeling that she was no longer needed, would vanish. 'We managed to assure him,' his mother says, 'that everything was all right, that I would always be there to pick him up from school.'

Martin was never to be offered that sort of reassurance. When the blue Austin that had brought him to boarding school carried his mother through the gates where he had been left, without any preparation or explanation, at the age of five, he was not to see her again for many weeks. He felt abandoned, absolutely alone, as if he had been flung over the edge of a precipice into a never-ending void. Even now, when he is a judge in his early sixties, he still sobs hysterically if his wife goes away on any trip more substantial than a visit to the local supermarket. Each time she leaves, he is carried back to those childhood feelings of utter panic.

Most boys are able to overcome, at least partially, this fear of losing the woman who is dearest to them. Mother's repeated re-appearances reassure him that she *will* always come back. It is sometimes said that he 'internalises' an image of her, so that he imagines her to be with him even when she has been gone for a while. Only when her absence is extended beyond what he has come to expect will he be thrown back into the same sense of panic that blighted his earliest months and years.

The boy wants his mother to be reliable, stable and compliant, never threatening to disturb the parameters of his life or undermine his sense of security. That is why any deviation from the norm can disturb him, and why boys sometimes come to see themselves as mothers' moral policemen. Sean, for example, remembers an occasion when he was nine and went to the pub with his mother. While he sipped at his orange juice, she knocked back a few lagers. The alcohol went to her head and she got up on a table to sing. Seeing his mother behave like that, Sean was disgusted and reported the incident to his father, who laughed and said there was nothing wrong with it. 'I just felt it was really common,' was Sean's reaction. 'I felt my mother was a cut above the rest. I couldn't see why she wanted to stand up and sing in front of these people.'

Bryan remembers with some remorse how he behaved when, at the age of eleven, he discovered that his mother had lied in reporting that she had given up smoking. He could smell the fumes coming out from the toilet to which she retreated after each meal, and he would then find her butts floating in the bowl. Although at the time his father regularly came home drunk and behaved in an intolerable way, it was his mother's relatively harmless dishonesty that distressed him much more. In fact, it was *because* his father had gone so far beyond the pale, that Bryan needed his mother to toe the line. 'My father causing embarrassing scenes was just accepted, but this perfect, lovely person smoking really upset me. My mother was supremely predictable really. This massive deceit came out of nowhere. I felt very bitter about it.'

By seeking to control his mother, the boy aims not only to ensure a stable environment for himself, but also to acquire a sense of his own power over others. He may find that he can manipulate her with a happy smile and a few gentle words. He may go along with what she asks, listening to her words and obeying her commands, in order not to break the bond of affection that exists between them. He may scream, shout and insist, making life hell for mother until she buckles under and does what he demands. Or he may act out his own fears and seek to stimulate in her the terror that he feels inside, running off into the park or stalking across the fields, waiting for her to come frantically in search of him.

If the boy manages to convince himself that his mother is there for him, and also finds that he can influence her behaviour towards him, he will develop confidence in his own powers. Again there is a paradox here. It is because there is somebody else ready to serve him, and because he knows he can make her work for him, that the boy is able to develop his capacity to do things for himself.

The negotiation between mother and son is not an easy one, since both of them are in the play of enormous contradictory pulls. Although the boy wants to establish his autonomy, he also recalls the bliss of infancy, fantasising about it as a time when he experienced himself as the sun around which the rest of the world rotated. He longs to sink back into that state of dependency, when all his needs were taken care of, and yet he also wants to pull away, to assert his autonomy and his potency.

Mothers too are divided between their nostalgia for the past and their anticipation of future pleasures. Although it is sometimes argued that, if left to themselves, all women would keep their children forever in nappies, in reality most have many good reasons for wishing their sons off their backs. The pleasure to be had from a cooing little boy is rather limited in the long term, and a mother might well look forward to the prospect of gazing upon a strong, responsible and capable male who can make her feel proud of his achievements. Whether she wants her boy to succeed at his schoolwork, box his way to the regional light-weight championships or earn more money than his father, she must urge him away from her skirts. The interests of mother and son are not opposed, then, but they are difficult to disentangle. Both feel a strong pull towards union and an equally powerful push towards separation. Tensions arise when the mother pulls harder than the son can bear, and he will respond usually by forcefully breaking away.

When Rebecca's boy was ten months old, she began to think he was a little clinging, and wanted to see if she could do something about it. She held on to him tight for every minute of the day and prevented him from waddling on his own to the door as the newspaper came through the letterbox, or going out with his father when he took the dog for a walk across the fields. 'It was to develop an understanding,' she explains, 'that being stuck to his mother all the time was the last thing he would find desirable.' Only two days of this treatment were necessary before her son became determined to escape. Her clinging caused him to pull away.

But what Rebecca tried as an experiment, many mothers do for real, without any capacity to respond when their sons insist that they need more space, more freedom, more opportunity. If she feels unhappy, unloved or anxious, she will hang on to her son and never want to let go. Instead of giving him a sense of inner security, she seems to take it from him. He feels that she is over-protecting him when he wants to go out and play with other kids. He feels weighed down by the anger or depression that he experiences in the house. The result is that what was once an enormously gratifying contact is now experienced as a set of oppressive chains. 'It felt like a sticky trap,' says Ted. 'It was too much. I felt I had to run away from home. I had to escape.'

Donald always felt that his mother was excessively anxious about his safety. When he went out to play football with other children, she wrapped him in the insignia of a mama's boy: hat, scarf and gloves. And when he wanted to stand by the window during a thunderstorm and enjoy the elements raging outside, she dragged him down into the cellar of their house and held him tightly to her. A forecast of bad weather would have her sweeping the cellar steps in preparation for the moment when they would need again to seek refuge there. As he grew up, Donald became steadily angrier with her for trying to exert so much control over him. 'The thing I most resent,' he says, 'is her not allowing me to sort of live my own life. I was rather weak then and I listened a bit much to her advice and warnings. Somehow I blame her for it.'

It is the experience of being constrained that arouses the boy to the greatest heights of fury. Whether he is held back by his own weakness or by his mother's restraining power, it is she who will become the receptacle of his anger and frustration. Any action that she takes can provoke him, whether she prevents him from exploring every corner of the house, from pulling down saucepans filled with boiling water or from poking his finger in the eyes of his baby sister. When, for example, two-year-old Leo's mother pulled him back from certain death under the wheels of a bus, he sank his teeth into her hands. When Oliver was nine and his mother was driving him to school one morning, he said to her (probably under the influence of one of the Stephen King novels he likes to read), 'You are the devil. I hate you. I wish that you were dead.'

A few months after this incident, I took Oliver out for a McDonald's hamburger to talk about his feelings towards his mother. Slightly to my surprise, he described her to me as the very image of moderate reasonableness. 'She doesn't smack me,' he said. 'She is not all that strict. She is easygoing.' Could this be the demonic mother he had attacked in the car? Had his mother got to him, and told him that he would not be fed for a week unless he gave her a good report? It seemed far more likely that Oliver had split his mother into the 'good' whom he loves unconditionally, and the 'bad' whom he feels free to hate, and it was the 'good' that he was now describing to me. Another son I interviewed said that whenever his mother became unpleasant, he used to think that some people had kidnapped her and were holding her, 'so that it was like two mums, the good one was being held captive and this was the nasty one'.

For as long as the boy remains in an intense relationship with his mother, it is useful for him to see his mother as two people – the gratifying and empowering mother who makes him feel secure, and the mother who frustrates him, whom he must demonise in order to encourage his break from her, and against whose might he can assert his own potency. The good mother justifies his love and dependency, while the bad inspires his quest for independence. Dividing mother up in this way enables a boy to move out into the world. If he can learn to hate his mother, he can leave her.

Some mothers work so hard to maintain the good-mother façade that their sons have to force them into the position of witch. During the three hours that I spent with Melissa, she came across as a woman so calm, so compassionate, so sensitive and yet solid that she evoked feelings in me which I can only describe as a form of love. It did not surprise me then to hear that her son Damian had to work at making her hateful. When he first started working at the age of fifteen, he wanted to save up for a hi-fi. Not trusting his own capacity for thrift, he put all his earnings in the care of his mother, whom he asked to pay him only a small allowance. Under no circumstances was she to respond to his request for more. A few days after making his first payment into her bank, he asked her for all the money. She refused. He started to yell at her: 'I want my bloody money. It's mine. You cannot steal my money. I am going to the police.' He then stormed out of the house, leaving his mother feeling quite awful about what she had been forced to do. When her son came back, he put his arms around her and thanked her for not giving in. He could treat her as his loving angel because she had played the role of witch so well.

The process of dealing with these images of mother and of woman stirs up strong feelings, and leaves numerous jarring images behind. She offers bliss, but pushes him away. She frustrates his omnipotence, but encourages him to develop self-confidence. She supplies love and yet tries to control him. She is a force to be feared, a power to be appeased, a creature to be worshipped. He learns that he must negotiate with her, doing whatever is necessary to ensure that he has the security needed to carry him forwards, countering his anxiety about the power she has over him, finding ways to sustain the love for him that he so needs.

Sons takes these fears and longings into all their future relationships. Can he be independent and yet lose himself in union with another? Is it possible for him to experience the feel of flesh, the joy of sucking, the pleasure of being stroked, without also re-awakening the terror, the anxiety and the frustration. Can he relive the time when he could stretch his hands towards his mother's bosom, open his mouth for the descending breast, then suck until he was sated and fell back towards sleep with a contented smile on his face, without undoing all the growth and the development that has been achieved?

The sight of his great-grandson feeding in his granddaughter's arms triggered in Archie memories of helplessness rather than of warm satisfaction. It is because their memories of the bad mother tend to push out those of the good that men are so often cautious and defensive in their relationships. They present themselves as natural pessimists, tending to remember the vicious row that took place before or after a party, rather than all the fun that was had. 'After the terrible struggle with this all-powerful mother' says psychoanalyst Christiane Olivier, 'how could men avoid opting for wariness in anything to do with women and their power, that power which must be held in check? How could they possibly not spend time setting limits to our world, shutting us away with our duties and responsibilities? How could a man's love for a woman be anything but ambivalent?'[3]

Men find it hard to establish a connection with others because they still carry with them this dread of mother; their fear that she will leave them, undermine them, withdraw her love. In this, the boy's experience is fundamentally different from any sister's. Whereas she separates from mother, always knowing that she will return to take up her mother's mantle, her mother's power, he does not have that guarantee. Not only can he never become like mother but, if he follows a heterosexual path, he must continually re-evoke the first bond with mother in his relationships to other lovers, replaying again and again the perilous dramas of his early life. 'If he lets her,' remarks feminist writer Dorothy Dinnerstein, 'she can shatter his adult sense of power and control; she can bring out the soft, wild, naked baby in him.'[4] The conflict between a mother and her son never ceases, it just moves to another battlefield.

What, after all, is the demand of those men who expect their wives to make a one-sided commitment to fidelity but the child's fear of loss and assertion of his need for mother so that he can feel confident enough to do just what he wants? 'If I always kept a reserve of women in addition to Hélène,' remarked French philosopher Louis Althusser in the autobiography he wrote to explain why he killed his wife, 'it was to ensure that, if by chance Hélène abandoned me or died, I would never for a single instant find myself alone.'[5] Why do some men demand such an abundance of attention and service from women, if it is not because they need constant reassurance that they will not be abandoned? Why do men not want to hear women swear or to see them having a good time unless it is for the same reason that Sean did not like his mother singing in the pub?

When men hypocritically assert that women should operate by different rules to them, is it not because they are still boys who see their wives as mothers upon whose reliability they depend?

CHAPTER THREE

The Lovelorn

When I phoned Hal to ask for an interview, he responded enthusiastically. I arrived at his house some mornings later, and had no sooner been ushered into his kitchen and turned on my tape-recorder than words started to tumble out of him. For an hour and a half, he sat holding a piece of buttered toast above the egg that he had boiled for his breakfast, ignoring my suggestions that he feed himself. His reluctance to eat made me feel gradually more uncomfortable, and his torrent of talk left me confused. Finally I called a halt to the interview, pleading that there was a malfunction on my tape machine, and suggested that we arrange a later meeting.

As the front door shut behind me, I felt that I had learned little about any sort of relationship that there might have been between Hal and his mother. He had told me a lot about her and just as much about himself, but not much about the two of them together. I wondered if this revealed the tenuousness of the connection between them. Had she been a looming presence rather than a mother who was available to her son? Hal had told me some of his earliest 'memories', which were almost certainly projections back from later experience, and these did seem to support such a theory. He recalled crawling along his bed and reaching up to his mother's breasts in the hope of being fed, only to find himself pushed away. He also spoke about an occasion when he fell out of his crib, to be picked up and returned to his blankets without the hug for which he had longed.

All his life, Hal suggests, his mother has tried to keep him at a distance. When he was five and just learning to write, she suffered a nervous breakdown which led to her being placed in a mental hospital in New York City some one thousand miles away: she travelled so far in order to have a proper break from her husband and four sons. 'She became a stranger to me,' Hal says. 'I don't think I saw her as my mother.' And when she returned home, she installed air conditioning in her room, with the intention, as Hal saw it, of excluding the noise of her four boys as they played in the garden just outside. When she wanted to speak to any one of them, she used the buzzer system in the house. 'If you heard this thing buzz,' Hal recalls, 'it meant that she was asking whoever was in that room to come to her room. And generally, it was not a nice thing.'

Freud wrote that a man who was his mother's darling retained 'throughout life the triumphant feeling, the confidence in success, which not seldom brings actual success along with it'. The obverse is true also. If a boy does not feel that anyone particularly cares for him, that he is special to at least one of his parents, he can never develop real self-worth. If he could see things as they really are, the boy would recognise that his mother is depressed, sad, anxious, or distracted for some other reason. Since he cannot do this, his first thought is more likely to be that there is something wrong with *him*, some deficiency that makes him unworthy of more than an occasional burst of mother love. He may try to win her over, to cajole her into providing the attention that he craves, but he is unlikely to have much success. It is almost impossible to throw off this sense of worthlessness once it has become entrenched. However much he achieves, however many people tell him he is wonderful, he will never find the sense of ease that he seeks. The Lovelorn may learn to cover up his lack of self-esteem, but he can never experience deep self-confidence.

It is difficult, though, to know how a child who was not being severely deprived might conclude that he was being denied a sufficient share of love. It cannot be that there is some fixed quantity of hugs, caresses and soothing words that every boy needs if he is to grow up feeling sure of himself. How would he assess whether he had received his quota? How could he know that others were getting so much more? What happens is that either he sees one of his siblings being preferred over him, or he experiences a mother who is occasionally effusive in her affections, but more often cool, distant and remote. He comes to know what it is that will make him feel good, but he does not seem to obtain very much of it. A mother need not be especially cruel or remiss for her son to feel that some quality is missing from his life. 'He seems so desperately hungry for love,' the exhausted mother of one six-year-old boy once said to me.

Like Hal, Victor claims to have 'memories' from earliest childhood of his mother's inadequate care. He recalls her breasts as 'hanging, sagging, slightly wrinkled and white', and suggests that feeding from them was not a satisfactory experience. Again, this must be an extrapolation from later experience. 'I don't know what she really felt about us,' Victor says. 'She must have loved us really, but she seemed so far from really knowing how to love someone.' He remembers the sense of rejection he felt whenever his mother sounded off about the 'bloody children', apparently blaming them for everything that had gone wrong in her life.

Hearing his mother's complaints, sensing the deficiency in her love, the Lovelorn tries to find a way of shifting her depressed mood. Victor did what he could to make his mother behave in a more satisfactory way towards him, sometimes getting up before the rest of the family and making breakfast just for her. It seemed to him that, on those occasions, she barely uttered a word of thanks, and her attitude towards him shifted not a jot. He eventually gave up trying.

Many therapists are Lovelorn sons who have turned the healing of mother into their lifelong preoccupation. One distinguished psychoanalyst once recalled to me how his mother's grumbles about her husband's foibles and failures inspired his attempt to do something for the two of them, but his best efforts never seemed to have any effect. 'If I can't make them better,' he eventually concluded, 'I'll make the world better. You can't make anything better without understanding it, so I'd better start understanding it. That has gone on ever since.' When Hal was young, he enthusiastically embraced the nickname Mr Fixit that his mother gave him. 'I fix tape-recorders,' he says, 'I fix people, I fix relationships, I fix families.' Now in his early forties, Hal is a social worker and family therapist who still tries to persuade his mother, who lives on the other side of the Atlantic, that she can now give up her visits to the psychiatrist.

A Lovelorn boy works hard to win his mother's loving approval, as a step towards improving his self-confidence. When his attempts are frustrated, he is likely to be made more despondent still by observing a lack of love in the relationship between his parents. If only he could see them being intimate and affectionate with each other, then he could at least feel that the love for which he craves was available somewhere. As it is, there is nothing to inspire this hope.

Victor told me that he had absolutely no idea what had once brought his mother and father together. He described his father as being of 'no use to anybody', and referred to his parents as 'just two pieces of furniture who stayed together'. He cannot remember witnessing from them any display of affection. For Hal, the problem between his parents was expressed in the design of the house that had been built for them as a wedding present: a long, low building which had his study at one end and her room at the other. The two of them tended to communicate by intercom or telephone, which echoed Hal's experience of his mother summoning her children for a reprimand by pressing that loud buzzer.

The Lovelorn son, then, lives in an environment that is deficient in emotional warmth. His efforts to improve this situation fail, leaving him convinced that he is powerless to change things. The lack of overt affection from his parents causes his hope for love to dwindle further. And yet he does have enough good experience of mother to know what pleasures there are to be found in a woman's arms. While his nursing was never satisfactory, it at least left him with a taste of what might have been. Realising that mother cannot satisfy his needs, the Lovelorn son sets out hungrily and precociously in search of someone else who will.

Some Lovelorn sons discover a relative or grandparent who will provide real affection. During the period when his mother was in hospital, Hal was lucky enough to have access to a loving nurse, and a grandmother who treated him as her favourite among the four brothers, allowing him sometimes to come into the double bed that she shared with grandpa. He relives that experience every night by sleeping, as did grandpa and grandma, on a double bed made from two singles that have been pushed together, on which he finds his way to a favourite position, on the crack between them. His nostalgia is so great because his mother's return blocked such easy access to the pleasures once experienced from grandma, and because her warmth emphasised the frigidity of his mother, the woman from whom he sought parental love.

Eventually, though, most Lovelorn sons have to undertake the frightening task of seeking someone outside the immediate family circle who will give them love. They may turn to neighbours, teachers or the parents of friends, but they are hardly likely to obtain from them the sort of sustained affection that they need. Victor claims that he was hardly out of nappies before he was fantasising about being cuddled by a visiting aunt who seemed to him so warm and so lovely that he imagined himself to be in love with her. 'It was pretty painful and hurt me a lot,' he says, adding that 'there was definitely a sexual side to it.'

Such a passion is bound to be scary and unsatisfactory, because the boy is playing with emotions he does not understand, directing his affections to people who are not primed to respond. Recognising how dangerous is the territory into which he has moved, the Lovelorn son is driven back to his fantasies, where he will often create an imaginary mother who can satisfy his longing. Whereas most boys split their real mother into 'good' and 'bad', the Lovelorn essentially writes her off as a failure and focuses instead on a woman who is all 'good' – all-loving, ever-attentive, nurturing, soft, kind. The Lovelorn may search for this paragon throughout his life but he will never find her; for his erotic desire is focused on an idealistic fantasy, the ideal mother of his dreams who will never be nasty or cruel and never provide him with any reason for giving her up.

A story that Hal told me illustrates how powerfully this image of the ideal mother can live on in the penumbra of consciousness. He was at a Hippie Fair where he went to take a steam bath. A woman sitting there caused the image of his mother to flash before his eyes. 'I found her exceptionally attractive,' he recalls. 'I talked to her. There was something going on that was interesting. Then she said that she had to go. She threw on her clothes and started running. I did not know who she was or if I would ever see her again. I ran with her through the rain. She turned to look at me. She was the image of my mother.' What excited Hal was the physical image of his mother in the person of someone who might have been attentive and loving to him in a way that his mother never was.

It can be seen how difficult it is for the Lovelorn, whose romantic yearnings have been for so long focused on such an imaginary woman, to grapple with a real relationship. He has not grown up struggling with the ups and downs of a mother's feelings towards him, learning to negotiate her moods and taking the knocks of her reproaches; instead he has lived in the hazy glow of a perfect love with a woman modelled according to his ideal desires. His imaginary mother never provokes him or challenges him, never urges him to the sort of achievements on which he might build his self-esteem. Having never had a real relationship of any sort, he will often find that he does not know how to deal with a woman, either emotionally or sexually. His inexperience, timidity and lack of realism are likely to make most women turn and run.

Unlike so many other men, the Lovelorn recognises that he has a problem with relationships, not so much because women tell him so (they tell many other men as well), but because he is sufficiently lacking in arrogance to hear what they are saying. He is also very much aware of his own fears about going too close to someone and exposing himself to the risk of further rejection. 'There is always,' one Lovelorn said to me of his romantic lethargy, 'this feeling that she won't like me, she won't want to talk to me.'

Unable to make any sort of approach, the Lovelorn will gratefully accept almost any woman who offers herself to him. Instead of seeking someone who might satisfy his emotional needs, enabling him to grow and develop, he resigns himself to making do with whatever is easily available. She may be violent, a drug addict, someone chronically faithless, but if she expresses desire for him, he will fall for it. That does not mean, though, that he will feel confident enough to work at the relationship, to stop himself from continuously trying to break away, which is the only way he knows of taking control. 'They kind of get upset,' one Lovelorn said to me, 'that I don't give and get close to them. I want to be in love, to have great sex and all that kind of thing. But looking at myself realistically, I don't think it is going to happen.' Although intelligent, affable and good-looking, he had found that the problems associated with his Lovelorn state were insuperable.

For Victor, sex with other people has never matched up to

his masturbatory fantasies, and he often wonders why things were so much easier then. 'It was raw sex,' he wistfully recalls. 'You could do anything you liked, with anyone you liked. I would just see someone, get a hard on, go home and wank.' The reality of his eventual seduction by a woman some twenty years older than himself was, by contrast, a little 'disappointing'. Things were no better when he was fixed up with a prostitute as a birthday present. 'She lay there,' Victor recalls, in the flat, emotionless tone he adopts throughout our interview. 'There was some music on. She was singing to the music. I fucked her. It was not exciting.'

I was talking to Victor shortly after he had finished a three-year relationship: his girlfriend walked out on him when she discovered that he had been sleeping with someone else. 'I cannot remember,' he says, 'the reason why I had that affair. Something was not right. I didn't feel very safe.' This statement turned out to have been somewhat disingenuous. Victor felt upset by his girlfriend telling him that he could not satisfy her sexually, and, as he experienced it, lecturing him on how he might increase her pleasure. He seemed able to talk with me about this, but reluctant to acknowledge its relevance to the break-up of their relationship.

In contrast to Victor, Hal was willing to talk and talk and talk about his sexual problem. (He was also happy to tell me about the sexual malfunctions that afflicted his three brothers.) His first wife, though, did not find this loquaciousness took them very far towards tackling his problems with touch and with sustaining himself in intercourse. When he suggested that they went for help, she initially replied that he had to deal with this one on his own.

They did eventually seek assistance together, but the disparity in their approach led to her short-circuiting each attempt they made. She walked out of a Masters and Johnson-style therapy session because she hated the idea of a man telling her how to have sex. When Hal's parents suggested the use of a vibrator, she replied that she had not married 'a machine'.

Finally, in complete exasperation, she quit marriage guidance, declaring that Hal would have to deal with *his* problem by *him*self. She started telling friends who had come round for drinks about her husband's sexual inadequacies, which stirred in him immense embarrassment and irritation.

It was not only the persistence of their sexual difficulties that caused Hal's wife to become so vexed with him, but also a more general sense that it was impossible for her to connect with him emotionally. There was nothing that Hal could not intellectualise, but he would never tell his wife how he felt, nor do anything to convince her that he *did* have strong feelings for her. Much of the behaviour that Hal describes to me suggests a woman vainly trying to get through to her husband. At one point, she asked how he would react if she slept with a mutual friend. Instead of saying what it was he would feel, he said non-committally, 'I think you should make the decision yourself. It should not be based on how I feel about it.'

Hal's wife did, though, find a way to extract an emotional reaction out of him. They were attending a Blues festival, and Hal was at the wheel of the car, waiting in a queue outside the entrance. When Hal's wife asked him for the tickets so that she could go inside, he felt upset that she did not want to wait with him and told her that they would not be able to find each other if they separated now. When she tried to tug the tickets out of his hand, he thumped her. 'I have been waiting two years for you to do that,' she said to him later, as she pulled him towards her for a bout of ecstatic love-making. She had not wanted to be hit, but any experience of spontaneous feeling seemed like a breakthrough.

The Lovelorn's sexual problems express his lack of self-confidence, and his more general difficulty with understanding his feelings. Because there was never anybody there to whom he could confess what he was going through, he never learned to recognise his emotions or to articulate them. 'I feel a certain emotional deadness, as if I am living a bit of a lie,' remarked one Lovelorn. 'I am not even sure what love is. I have never been sure. I say I love my wife, but I am not sure that I do. I am very drawn to her and very fond, but when I tell her that I love her, I don't really know exactly what I am saying. I don't feel totally comfortable in saying it.'

What rarely finds full expression is the rage that the Lovelorn son feels against his mother. It seems foolish to express anger at someone from whom one still forlornly hopes to secure love. Later, when that hope has died, there seems little point in saying anything at all. Never having a real relationship with mother, he does not learn that it is possible to be angry and to be loving at the same time. 'I am always,' says Victor, 'going to have some sort of deep resentment about it. It seems so unnecessary to have put anyone through all that crap. The least I can do is to own that anger and say "Fuck you".' I have the sense, though, that it is only because his parents are both dead that he can be so upfront about his feelings. Hal seems to have deflected his anger on to the house that he feels shaped his mother's attitude to him and to the rest of the world. 'I like the house,' he says, 'but I feel that I would probably have had a better life if it had burned down.'

The Lovelorn is also angry with himself: he carries still the sense that there must be something wrong with him. He is often a drifter who can never settle to one thing because he lacks the confidence to carry it through. Failing to develop his full potential, he is aware of his stunted capacities, his emotional limitations, the difficulties he has in forming relationships, his sexual problems and the lack of any direction to his life. It is no coincidence that two of the Lovelorn sons described in this chapter are both expatriates living in London. Victor, who is in his twenties, lives in England because that is where he ended up, not because he ever wanted to stay there. He might consider moving on soon, he tells me, but not to go back to New Zealand. Then again, he might. 'I certainly have no desire now,' he says. 'I can't be bothered with it really.' Hal, who grew up in Georgia, says he loathes job titles that would pin him down. He has been, in his time, a designer, a chef, an electrician and a businessman, before becoming a social worker.

While many Lovelorn sons do stay closer to the parental home, they too quest largely in vain for love of a sort that they have never known. They will move from job to job, from relationship to relationship, often ending up in therapy, talking about what they might be looking for, but never quite becoming confident enough to define fully the nature of their quest.

CHAPTER FOUR

Crossing the River

The bawling infant whose penis earns him the title 'boy' still has a long way to go before he can call himself a 'man'. Physical maturity is taken care of by a battery of hormones, but what drives his psychological development?

During my research for this book, I kept coming across the same account of a boy's journey to manhood, which goes something like this: he starts out on the 'feminine' bank of a broad river, basking in the delights of his mother's love and living in a sort of feminine haze. The experience is so pleasurable that he would happily stay there forever, were it not for the fact that his father is on the other side (and if he does not have one, he will imagine that he has), summoning him to cross, urging him to 'separate' from mother and to repudiate everything that is 'female'. The waters that divide the masculine from the women's realm are turbulent and his mother exerts a strong pull, but the boy's terror of being swallowed up in femininity is so great that he beats back his mother and sets out on a slow and difficult journey across the river. 'Somewhere on the other side of the mother,' writes Carol Lee, 'in a land different from her feminine soil, there is a condition called "being male" or "masculinity" which a boy has to find.'[1]

This account assumes that there exist two distinct worlds, male and female, and that a boy has to move from one to the other as he matures. The differences between the sexes are seen as much more important than the similarities, and there is something fixed about the qualities ascribed to each. 'Masculinity' is not what each boy decides to make of himself, but a condition that he has to attain. He becomes what he is not through his relationships with individuals, who happen to be male or female, but by embracing as best he can a certain concept of gender. This is not an accurate way to describe the boy's development of his ideas about 'masculinity'.

It is misleading, for a start, to suggest that the boy's early condition is 'feminine'. It is true that he is usually very close to his mother, and he will generally be dependent upon her for emotional and physical sustenance. He may also tend to assume for a time that he is a creature like her, so that he is perplexed by the discovery that she does not possess a penis like his (or something rather more impressive). But in his earliest years he knows much too little about the difference between the sexes for him to conceive of himself as being on one side or the other of the great divide.

His situation could more accurately be described as one of confusion, or gender amorphousness, in which he struggles to make sense of his vague awareness that the world is divided into two sexes, and that he will eventually have to fit into one particular category. From the age of about a year, every child has a sense of himself or herself as being of one sex rather than the other, but this recognition does not mean very much. 'The likely thing,' says child psychotherapist Paul van Heeswyck, 'is that there are all sorts of images playing in his head all the time, like a sort of film, a constant backdrop. He can think of himself as a girl, as a boy, as all sorts of things.' The baby boy does not seek to achieve the adult destiny imposed upon him by his genitals – he would probably rather avoid being forced into choosing at all.

The Crossing the River myth suggests that, were it not

for some outside intervention, the boy would stay forever by his mother's side, helplessly dependent upon her. This implies that all women are naturally clingy, fails to recognise the boy's own yearning to 'separate' himself from the woman who once fed him, stroked him, nursed him and protected him, and suggests that his task is inherently different from a girl's. In fact, both sexes must prove that what mother once did for them, they can do for themselves. Some mothers are co-operative in this project, encouraging their children in every way they can, while others, being reluctant to surrender control over their beloved children, put up all sorts of obstructions. Some boys and girls also receive backing from their fathers, others do not. It is not the desire to be a 'man' that drives the boy away from mother, it is the urge to become an individual (albeit a male one).

Nor is the family background of most boys likely to encourage the view that there is some neat distinction to be drawn between the personal attributes of men and women, and that the male position is inherently more desirable. The boy is just as likely, for example, to see a tired and debilitated man returning from work to slump before the television as he is an energised and forceful figure striding through the door and asking for his dinner. He may have been appalled by the sight of his father cowering on the ground after unsuccessfully intervening in a fight but recall his mother managing the family budget, running the hire-purchase account at the local store, hanging wallpaper and painting walls.

When Michael, who is now a judge, was a small boy some fifty years ago, he experienced his mother as someone strong and dynamic. She had risen from humble origins as the daughter of a drunken village blacksmith to become a doctor's wife, running her husband's practice during his periods of debilitating illness. His aunts were similarly impressive. One started off as a house-maid but rose to become, during the Second World War, a colonel in the American army, with responsibility for welfare operations in occupied Germany;

another was a successful businesswoman who, after running the sewing machine department of a large store, began building up a property empire. Michael was much more impressed by the roles that women offered him than by the examples set by his ailing father, his uncle who drove buses or another who had become a blacksmith like his father. His mother also made clear how low a view she had of her brothers: when they doffed their caps to her outside the church, she ignored them. His drive to manhood could hardly be based on the assumption that all power and dynamism rests in the male.

If mother is not some drudge chained pathetically to the kitchen sink but instead a powerful, vital being who encourages her sons to develop their independence, her boy does not need to 'repudiate' her example so that he can 'identify' with his father in order to grow into an effective and forceful individual. There is no reason why he should make any sort of radical choice between the models that his parents offer, since he can pick and choose between them. A host of inputs can be taken in and processed to determine whether a particular boy will become a bully or a wimp, a swot or a sportsman, as he finds his personal answer to the question, 'What does it mean that I am a male?'

'Masculinity' is not something that can be sought for, described and analysed. It is a question that is posed by the boy's discovery of his biological difference, and one to which there are many different answers. The boy's particular formulation will emerge out of the experience he has of his parents, and the particular problems that are thrown up by his relationship to them. Which of his parents does he feel most drawn to? Which of them does he find the most impressive? Does he feel sympathy with a father who appears weighed down by his mother's emotional demands, or angry at a father who does not stand his ground? He will try to develop the attributes that are useful to him, rather than following some course predetermined by his biological sex.

Arnold and Simon grew up in a small village by the sea, two boys in a family of five children. Their father was a farm labourer, and money was always tight, but their mother could make it go a long way. By growing her own vegetables, saving carefully and avoiding unnecessary expense, she was able to manage on the sort of income that would have pushed many people into debt. Because she always stayed close to the house – ironing, cleaning and spending time with the children – both have warm memories of mother being 'always there' for them. But as they came into their teens their parents started to quarrel, father taking the view that the boys should leave school and start bringing in some money, while their mother wanted them to study and 'better' themselves. The boys aligned themselves on different sides of this argument, their attitudes reflecting identifications that had begun to form much earlier in their lives.

Arnold, the younger of the two, took up what one might see as the 'traditional' male position against his mother. He had long felt resentful about the special attention that his brother received from her, considering that his own qualities were under-valued in comparison: he was sometimes described as a 'right little handful' or a 'silly boy'. It particularly upset him that, whereas his brother's academic achievements were lauded highly, his mother never came to watch his sporting activities, and took no particular notice when he became captain of rugby or regional athletics champion. This made him sympathetic to his father, whose contribution to the family budget did not seem to win him very much respect.

Arnold began a campaign to clarify the differences between himself and his mother. Whereas she got up at four in the morning to do the laundry, he refused to be dragged from his bed until it was almost time for the school bus to arrive. Whereas she spent her days keeping house, he railed at the duties he was meant to perform: washing dishes, cleaning shoes and chopping sticks. And as he started to side with his father, he also began wanting to be *like* his father. When the weekend came around and he had an opportunity to go out and help dad finish the milking, all his early-morning sloth would disappear. He wanted to escape his mother's regime, to get out in the world and start working. 'I desperately wanted to grow up,' he recalls.

While Arnold expresses admiration for his father, and measured contempt for his mother, his brother takes the opposite perspective. Simon always had far more respect for his mother's abilities as a money-manager than for his father's performance as a money-earner. During her convalescence from a difficult birth, he showed how highly he considered his mother's skills by taking over responsibility for the shopping and for paying the household bills. 'He would not,' his mother recalls with pride of her ten-year-old, 'let any shopkeeper get away with charging him too much.' Now a medical consultant managing an annual budget of £9 million and running his own business at the same time, Simon provides his parents with the money they need to live in a comfortable house, drive a good car and take foreign holidays. In this way he demonstrates repeatedly how far he has risen above his dad, and how well he learned his mother's lessons in money management.

Is Simon less 'male' than Arnold as a result of this identification with his mother? Is he somehow 'damaged' by the warmth that he feels towards her? There was a period when Simon's disinterest in sport or rough-and-tumble made his father anxious that he might be gay, and he does have a less vigorous life than his brother, who is still enthusiastic about running and football. But to sustain the argument that Simon is somehow 'effeminate' would require upholding an extremely narrow definition of what 'masculinity' entails: he is, after all, ambitious, very successful, happily married and a contented father. He is not less male than his brother – he is just different.

The idea that there is a rigid dividing line between masculinity and femininity reflects men's anxiety about women's power, their sense of needing to retreat to a gender-defined reserve in order to protect themselves from danger. For those of this persuasion, the prospect that a boy might remain in the feminine realm with mother and not develop into a full 'male' appears truly terrifying. 'We believe,' psychoanalyst Robert Stoller remarks, 'that because little boys spent their most profoundly intimate experience up against a female body and psyche, they are at special risk of first identifying with the femaleness and then of not being able adequately to end that identification by the creation of masculinity.'[2]

Masculinity, though, is not the goal of the boy's development, rather it is a useful tool in the process. Newborn babes have no sense of who they are, why they are, what they should do with themselves. Their parents will probably tell them that they are male or female, but this means little to them. Nevertheless, a growing awareness of genital difference helps give them a sense of their having a separate existence. To the question 'Who am I?', the answer now comes back that 'I am a boy. I am not one of them.' 'For me to consolidate a sense of my own worth,' says child psychotherapist Paul van Heeswyck, 'I need to create a group of outsiders.'

For both boys and girls, the full realisation of what is entailed by their gender identity brings the pleasure of discovering what they have, and the trauma of acknowledging what they will never possess. The boy is forced to recognise that he will not be able to carry a baby as his mother did and consequently will never enjoy the sort of power that his mother has over him. This is a profoundly important realisation, and perhaps the whole of childhood is an attempt at coming to terms with what it might mean. The difficulty that adult men have in acknowledging their feelings on this subject is evident in the tendency to dismiss women as just baby-carriers while simultaneously worshipping them for their nurturing potential. As French psychoanalyst Christiane Olivier has observed, 'There is no end to the celebration in literature of our curved neck and bosom, our breasts, our tiny waist: in short all the things which men don't have and envy us for having.'[3]

From the start, accepting one's gender is a difficult task, which confronts boys and girls in different ways. Many boys are obsessed with toy cars. At the risk of coming across as a traditional follower of Freud, one might suggest that their preoccupation indicates a desire to find out what the hell they are going to use their penises for. Is it for hitting brother, ruining the paint work or sticking between some cushions? In their play, boys confront their existential crisis. What am I to do with this self that I have been given? Much angst has been experienced by mothers who see their girls playing with dolls while their brothers charge around the garden with toy AK47s in their hands. Is my boy going to turn into an awful macho brute? she asks herself. And she may respond with criticism of the 'sexist' behaviour rather than trying to understand what is going on in a boy's mind. It may be, though, that boys need to deal in this way with the discovery of the sexual identity which their genitals impose, and that allowing genuine concerns about the irresponsible behaviour of adult men to license heavy-handed parental interventions in a child's development is wildly inappropriate and likely to be very confusing for the child. There is a lot of time left for boys to develop nurturing skills, and for girls to learn that they can, in fact, aspire to run the country.

Because he knows his mother's life so intimately, and relatively little about his father's, the boy's discovery of her difference from him is in some ways the more shocking. 'For the girl,' writes journalist Angela Phillips, 'the moment of recognition is also a moment of power. For the boy, it is a moment of uncertainty.'[4] The knowledge that she will carry babies gives a girl a sense of (admittedly limited) purpose to her life, something that relates to her body which defines what she can become. The play with dolls is something meaningful that points a way towards a possible future. She has a sense of her role, in a way that the boy simply cannot, and this may explain why the quest for some definition of 'masculinity' is so fervent and intense, both in the playground and beyond.

It is because boys seek so anxiously for an answer to this question as to what masculinity might mean that they do not sit around talking with their mates but set about trying to *do* something. Whether it is kicking a ball around a football field, perfecting their game of chess or learning the trumpet, many boys seem to feel the need for an all-absorbing form of activity. 'I used sport as a direction-finder,' one man said to me. 'The basic thrill of it was that I was rather good at it. It came naturally. But I always felt that one day my personality would depend on things other than sport.'

The father's position is often represented as the more desirable because it indicates the possibility of living a life apart from the mother with whom her children have been landed. His long periods of absence may give to father's non-domestic life the charm of the exotic unknown, but that is not much help to his son in working out what it means to be a male. Whether dad is loafing around the house between visits to the dole office, marching off each morning with a briefcase in his hand, or slaving over a computer in an attic, it is never quite clear what he is for. When father is around, the boy may well try to join in his activities so as to find out what this male business is all about, but all he can really know is that he is not going to be a mother. When he reports his wish to become a train driver, an astronaut or a jungle explorer, it is because he senses that he has been sent on a journey without any clear destination. He is expressing a desire to escape the chains that bind him to others, not to be like daddy, who in most cases is none of these things.

The prospect of maternity not only provides a girl with a more secure sense of her future, albeit one that she will hopefully want to enlarge at a future date, it also offers her the possibility that she may experience through a male child the gender role that she has been compelled to abandon. It is because the boy does not experience his paternal function in the same way (when a man says that he would like a girl child rather than a boy, it is often assumed he has some sinister object in mind) that he can find it so much more difficult to accept his biological destiny. While many women want access to men's advantages, there is no equivalent to the obsessive need that some men have to experience the feminine position by wearing women's clothes or changing their sex through surgical intervention. This is partly, of course, because a woman can don suit, tie and brogues without attracting any special attention, and without feeling that the statement she is making endangers her sexual identity. It has also been observed that women who fantasise engaging in sex from the male side tend to visualise themselves as women with a penis, not as men.

It is because the boy finds it hard to accept that he will never be able to do what mother does that he has so passionately to argue the case for his superiority. This involves dismissing girls and the softer sort of boys as 'wimps' and 'sissies', and embracing the fantasies offered by popular culture so that he imagines himself rescuing POWs from Vietnam, negotiating peace treaties with warring parties and taking over the controls of plunging aeroplanes. But far from feeling secure in their claims to power, boys scream so loudly and defend their patch so resolutely because they fear for the consequences if they were to let women get too close. Suspecting that they could not withstand a direct attack, they treat the demarcation between men and women as their Maginot Line.

This form of gender rancour can only be dissolved by bringing into consciousness the desire of men and women not to be confined to one sex or another. While boys and girls mostly learn to carry their assigned sex roles with a sort of pride, they also have a residual desire to be the other. It is not so much that they want to change sex, just that they pine for the freedom to be both, to avoid having to choose. It is this yearning that shapes the patterns of our emotional attachments, and later our sexual desires. Envying what the other has that we cannot have, we try to close the gap in our relationships with lovers and partners.

What the case studies in this book show is the continuing strength of gender's grip on the way people view each other. The sexing of an infant significantly influences the expectations that others have for him. The different experiences that he has of his male and female parents shape the patterning of his terrors and his desires, so that these childhood feelings will come to determine the whole pattern of his emotional life: the degree to which he is capable of loving and getting close. Too many sons are never given the means to deal with the insecurities that give rise to the belief that boys and girls belong to different species.

The next chapter looks at the Wild Men, those who suffer most acutely from the ills of masculinity.

CHAPTER FIVE

Wild Men

If the Lovelorn feels that his mother does not truly care for him, the Wild Boy has no awareness that she ever might have done. He behaves as if he were totally on his own and had never been offered any form of emotional support. He is like a blind sheep who charges into dry stone walls while his fellow beasts pass in relatively good order down a country lane. Feeling that there is no one upon whom he can rely, he strives with passionate intensity to assert his independence, lashing out at parents, siblings and others in displays of strength. He longs for comfort but, sensing the impossibility of relief, he runs away from every safe place that is offered. His arms always flailing, he cannot ever settle or easily accept whatever helping hand is offered to him. Carried ever onwards by his obsessions, he hurtles towards self-destruction.

The reason why he behaves in this way is largely a mystery. His lack of basic trust seems to have much more to do with what is going on in his own head, than with anything that could have happened in his dealings with mother or others. Some argue that there must be some simple genetic explanation for his antisocial ways. Others consider that such cases provide evidence for the view that male brains are wired differently from the female, in a way that makes all boys less skilled at forming relationships, and Wild Boys particularly so. It seems more likely that a mix of environmental and chromosomal forces make some boys feel a sense of frantic insecurity. The mother's response to this bawling obstreperousness may improve things or cause his behaviour to deteriorate, but it cannot fundamentally alter his condition.

'I am in awe of Roderick,' Ailish says, 'because I cannot see how I produced him.' Almost from the moment of his birth, she says, he was an 'angry, angry thing'. As a child, he would scream and cry, refusing to be pacified. The arrival of a sister made his behaviour worse. Obsessively jealous, Roderick would repeatedly push her off his mother's lap. The more independent she became, the harder he would hit her. He once pushed her down the stairs so hard that she cracked her head and passed out.

Roderick seemed to lack any sense of control or restraint. When bashing pegs into holes, he kept on hitting them until the toy was broken. At playschool and later, he delighted in terrorising other children, sometimes chasing them around the playground with a spade held high above his head. He would stand at the top of the school staircase, block the way for the other children and then, when a large enough number had accumulated in front of him, he would push. He also tried to burn the school down by scattering Ajax onto a pile of toilet paper and setting it alight. Teachers regularly threatened to quit if Roderick stayed in their class.

Ailish rarely felt in any personal danger from her son's violence, although on one occasion he did raise a steel bar over her and seemed about to bring it down. 'I felt frightened and horrified,' she recalls, 'that this small boy could pick on his mother, who would have done anything she could to make him happy.' For most of the past 22 years, though, she has been asking herself what made her son turn out this way, anxiously reviewing Roderick's history in a search for clues.

Ailish recalls the pain she felt when a clumsy doctor ran wires up her womb to monitor the condition of the foetus and wonders whether that process may have caused distress to her gestating son. 'Maybe,' she says, 'his birth was more traumatic than it should have been.' She has read about possible links between various food additives and hyperactivity. She sometimes wonders too whether it will turn out that he suffers from some sort of psychiatric condition that could be controlled with medication. And she also reflects upon the circumstances of his conception.

Ailish had borne another baby boy who died within a few days of his birth. In accordance with the thinking of the time, she was encouraged to try for a second child as soon as possible. With this in mind, and to recover from the shock of the first child's death, Ailish and her husband hired a Renault 4 and drove out into the Moroccan desert. They stayed in cheap hotels, the sort of places where the toilet was a hole in a floor that swarmed with cockroaches, and this insanitary environment seemed to explain the traveller's tummy that blighted Ailish's capacity for pleasure throughout most of the trip. As the couple passed through Taroudant, Ouarzazate and Marrakech, the opportunities for procreative sex were zero.

One day, they saw a black Citroen parked across the road. A man ran towards them screaming, '*Oh mon dieu! oh mon dieu!*' The reasons for his distress were soon apparent. A little shepherd boy lay where the car had hit him. Although his white face, with its tight blond curls, was undamaged, the boy was dead. '*Faites quelque chose!*' the wretched Frenchman implored. Ailish's husband turned the car around and drove towards the nearest town, where they reported the accident to the police before driving back to the scene. Passing by, they saw a group of women standing at the side of the road, around the body of the little boy. Weeping and wailing, they reminded Ailish of bent crows.

That night, Ailish and her husband stayed in a small cabin by a beach on the Atlantic Coast. It may have been the shock of the accident that caused Ailish's health to improve somewhat.

She ate lobster, drank some wine and, for the first time on that trip, made love with her husband. It was to be their only holiday coupling: the runs returned with the morning. Nine months later, Roderick was born. 'You are the little Moroccan boy,' she would sometimes say to her son, whom she liked to dress up in Arab costumes.

Did the grief that Ailish felt over her first-born communicate itself to her growing baby? Did these emotions combine with a series of clumsy medical intrusions into her womb to develop in Roderick a violent vexation, whose source he had no language to convey, no means to understand? It is certainly possible that his later behaviour was significantly influenced by pre-birth experiences.

Italian psychoanalyst Alessandra Piontelli has studied ultrasound film that shows babies in the womb and then followed up on their later personality development. Her conclusion is 'that certain pre-natal experiences may have a profound emotional effect on the child, especially if these pre-natal events are reinforced by post-natal experiences'.[1] She describes a three-year-old boy who was brought to see her because he seemed always anxious, and treated his mother as someone incapable of doing anything right, however hard she tried to calm him. 'You are a woman, and women are no good,' he would say to her. His troubled rages, inability to relax and constant alertness were traced by Piontelli back to pre-birth experiences. At three months, the doctors pronounced that he had died, but then his beating heart revealed that he was just alive. Because the placenta was inserted low, creating a high risk of miscarriage and massive bleeding, his mother had to stay in bed throughout the later pregnancy. At seven months, when she could bear her prone state no longer and went out for a walk, her son arrived. For some time afterwards, he clung to his mother's breasts as if for very life, monitoring her with his eyes, yelling and screaming if she moved away an inch. 'I felt that he treated me just like a sort of milking cow,' his mother said.[2]

Whatever the cause of his behaviour, the Wild baby's arrival is a shock to his mother, dashing her dreams of quiet contentment with a baby in her arms. A mother may think she is the calmest and gentlest woman in the world, but the arrival of such a screaming bundle is bound to test her patience. She will come to see child-rearing less as an experience to be enjoyed than as a task to be accomplished. The nature of her response will not turn a Wild Boy into somebody else, but it may well determine the form that his wildness takes.

When Rachel was pregnant, she would lie in bed and listen to a mother over the road yelling at her children, and think smugly that it would never be like that for her. She considered that she would be a brilliant mother whose children would reward the love she felt for them by being always well-behaved. The fact that she was anyway a calm, relatively unemotional person, convinced her that she would have no problems at all. This blissful fantasy was soon to be shattered.

Rather like Roderick, Rachel's boy was stroppy from the first days of his life. He would not sleep. He started to crawl long before other children. While they were lying in their prams, he was bumping into things. When they were sitting on the floor and playing quietly, he was banging with hammers and poking screwdrivers into other objects. For the first time in her life, Rachel knew what it was to feel anger. Quite inadequate to deal with the situation and fearful about the force of her rages, she remembers going into a room, picking up a bench and hurling it against the wall. 'It was the frustration of having a little one who did not want to do what you wanted him to do.'

Ailish too felt rage against her son. There was the afternoon when, unable to tolerate his screaming, she shook his basket in a red-hot fury, screaming 'shut up, shut up, I can't bear it'. There was the time when she broke a hairbrush on his back. And the circumstances of our interview almost convinced me that her barely-suppressed rage might provide some sort of explanation for her son's violence. When I rang to arrange my visit, Ailish told me that I was under no circumstances to open the cottage gate, since the bull terrier she kept might well go for me if I did. Throughout the interview, this beast kept trying to get between my legs so as to get a good sniff at my genitals. Did this dog express the aggression that simmered in the deepest recesses of Ailish's consciousness?

In the final analysis, this seemed unlikely. Any violence which Ailish inflicted upon her son seems always to have been caused by his extreme behaviour, so that it cannot be used as an explanation of that delinquency. Roderick describes his mother as having been incredibly restrained, given what he put her through. Far from behaving like a demonic harridan, she seems to have been a warm and attentive mother. Seizing the opportunity to relive her own childhood, she tried imparting to her children a sense of fun and adventure, taking them for walks in the woods and along deserted railways lines, organising parties and boating expeditions from their house by the river, putting herself out for her son and his friends. 'From the experience I have had of other people's mothers,' says Roderick, 'she was definitely one of the best.'

And yet, however hard she tried to provide a loving, containing environment for her son, Roderick never did feel secure. He saw enemies everywhere, and set out to defend himself by attacking others. He knew consciously that his mother felt kindly towards him, but all her efforts to pacify him could not prevail against his inner angst. It is this precocious, obsessive feeling that he must break away and protect himself which characterises the Wild Boy. Such behaviour can easily produce in his scorned mother a reaction that only makes things worse. His rages and threats may stir anger and aggression in her. Or her anxious attempt to make things better, her apparent weakness in the face of rage, may seem to confirm his feeling that he is without protection.

Sylvia's son Dominic almost died within days of being born. Again he was a first child, and the effect upon her was enormously to increase the anxiety that she felt about him. Her life was anyway in emotional turmoil. She had become estranged from her wealthy and domineering father who did not approve of the marriage or the pregnancy. And her husband was a depressive who had no capacity to cope with his new responsibilities, instead making extreme demands of his own upon her. These difficulties served to strengthen the you-and-me-against-the-world feeling that had already been fostered by the newborn infant's precarious hold on life.

Shortly after the arrival of her second child, a daughter, Sylvia went back to work, leaving her children in the care of a nanny. One day, when away from home, she received a message that one of her children had been in an accident. The feeling she had for her son was such that her question 'Which one?' expressed her hope that the victim would not be her beloved Dominic. In fact, a pan of boiling stock had drained upon his back, leaving him with scars that disfigure him to this day.

Dominic became used to his mother saying that she wanted to protect him, but repeatedly showing that she could not. He responded with violent tantrums, behaving so badly that some of his mother's friends said they would not come to the house if he was around, thus only pushing mother and son closer together. 'He was hurt enough,' she says, 'and so I would allow him to be naughty.' She let him make any demands on her that he wanted and tolerated his misbehaviour, but she could not prevent him from being assaulted by others. On one occasion, Sylvia's second husband was astonished to see her taking the four-year-old Dominic to the toilet before putting him to bed. 'Why can't he take himself?' he asked.

'If I don't, he will pee in his bed,' his mother defensively replied.

'No, he won't,' said his stepfather, 'and if he does, I am going to thump him.' When the blows rained down the next morning, Sylvia felt physically sick.

Having never felt able fully to trust his mother, the Wild

Man finds that he cannot empathise with the feelings of others. Driven by a fierce inner rage, he launches himself in violent acts of assertion against everyone else who comes within range. Unable to access his emotions, he strives to achieve mastery, to prove that he depends upon no one, that he is wholly autonomous and self-sufficient.

The Wild Man cannot bear anyone telling him what to do, or trying to confine him. Dominic's mother tried every sort of school for her son, from the kind of institution where pupils ran around in jeans and jumpers doing little organised work, to the sort where they wore caps and blazers, and always he ran away. His mother would tell him that he could only ride his bicycle on the pavement outside their house, and yet he would go for fifteen miles along the main roads that led to London Airport and watch the planes taking off for distant countries. Moved to hospital when his appendix burst, Dominic was unable to lie back, convalesce and be taken care of. He felt as if he was in jail, and discharged himself after only two days.

Roderick too seems to have had his heart set on escape from early on. He would throw a rage in response to the simplest demands, just being told that it was time for him to be wrapped in pyjamas, clean his teeth and go to bed. When he felt most unhappy he would let out a wail and declare, 'I want to be free, I want to be a bird.' Ailish says that her greatest fear for her son is that he might one day end up in prison, possibly for murdering a member of the family, where she is sure that he would go completely mad.

Yet although the Wild Man wants to flee any institution where he does not feel safe, this does not mean he has no pining for a structured, containing place. It is just that he is more frightened of being constrained than he is hopeful of finding such a refuge. But paradoxically the Wild boy can sometimes feel more at home within an apparently repressive institution than some of his contemporaries. Even Roderick, for example, responded to being in a school where the teachers were strict, the rules were clear and all the desks pointed in one direction, towards the blackboard. 'That actually did begin to work,' Ailish recalls.

Another Wild Boy, Eric was desperately insecure until he joined the cadet corps at school. When the emotional turbulence of his home life was replaced by the routine of the parade ground, he found many opportunities there to improve his sense of self-worth. He would polish his boots so that they gleamed and rise to the challenge of being forced by a vicious commander with a ruddy complexion and a booming voice to do 200 press-ups. 'I loved the cadets,' he says. 'Everything was structured and safe.'

Eric's later life has been a quest to find some other institution in which he could to hope to enjoy the same sense of security. He was turned down by the army for being too arrogant. He was accepted into the police, but persuaded by his mother that he would not be able to tolerate the likely corruption among associates and superiors. It was only after years of selling financial services and feeling wretched that he applied for his present, much more satisfactory, job as a customs officer.

'One of the things I like about it,' Eric says, 'is the machismo, the male-oriented side of it.' By working as a member of a team, pitting his wits against villains, he finds that he can lay aside any anxieties about his own security. Describing the challenge of surveillance and the rush of blood that precedes an arrest, he tells me how he loves being recognised by colleagues as someone who is good at his job and therefore trustworthy. 'You want to be somebody,' he says, 'that other people would be happy to follow through a door.'

It is because others see him as competent that Eric can now feel good in himself. Most Wild Men find it much harder to develop this sense of self-confidence, precisely because they are so deaf to the love and reassurance that others offer them. Feeling that mother is no use to them, they set out to break away, to prove to themselves that they can do everything which she once did for them. The Wild Man is obsessive in his quest for independence and autonomy.

Even at the age of six, Roderick was anxious to make it on his own. He started by selling his birthday presents from a blanket that he had laid out on the pavement beside his house, and went on from there to buying items at jumble sales which he sold on for a profit. As he speaks now about the business that he runs, it is possible to hear still the echoes of his lifelong struggle to break free of the 'power relationship' in which he felt himself to be enmeshed by his mother. 'Now that she doesn't control me,' he says, 'I am able to love her all the more.' But there is a large distance between the wish and the reality. Roderick still takes his washing home for mother to do and expects her to bail him out financially. On the day I saw Ailish, she was angry with him for coming late to pick up some dollars she had offered him, and consequently missing a flight to China.

When Roderick talks about his need for independence, which he calls 'self-created cultural autonomy', he sounds quite unhinged. 'If one wants to be a leader,' he goes on, 'one cannot have people who are controlling one, one must control oneself.' Sometimes he starts praising Hitler's war machine for its efficiency, and talks about exterminating the ignorant masses who might block his projects, which provokes Ailish into wondering whether she can any longer tolerate the behaviour of her son. 'A stage might come,' she says, 'when I would cut off from him.'

Nor does the Wild Man's need to break from mother mean that there is no residual desire to sink back into her arms. But much as he longs for a safe embrace, he does not believe that anyone can offer it to him, whether because he is unworthy, or because no one could have the capacity to tolerate his insatiable desires. He grows up, therefore, without any model of a trusting, mutual relationship with a woman. He longs for it, but fears it is impossible, that women will always reject him and destroy him. Unsurprisingly, his adult emotional life tends to be extremely chequered.

Roderick may strive for mastery in his work life, but his approach to women is one of prostration. He considers that it is the intensity of the feelings he reveals which has frightened off those he has sought to have as his girlfriends. 'There have been a number of occasions,' he says, 'when I have lost women due to the overwhelming largeness of the emotions I want to give to them. I want to sacrifice to them, to be almost like their slave.' Roderick's desire for servitude is an expression of his anxiety: he is willing to do anything that might keep them from turning against him or abandoning him. It is because of his fear that he abases himself before them. He takes women to the finest of restaurants and throws at them money he does not have. And when it all goes wrong, as it invariably does, he turns the fury that he once aimed at others towards himself. Feeling that his head is about to explode, he will drink alcohol mixed with furniture polish, slash his wrists and make cuts into his chest. Sometimes, his despair will make him feel as if he is going to plunge over the edge of the abyss into complete insanity.

It may be that this agony reflects aspects of his childhood experience, dating from those times when he found that his mother's love was not strong enough to pierce his anxious carapace and make him feel safe. He longs to make contact, and yet his past convinces him that his every attempt is doomed before he begins. He lacks any sense of reality about what women want, not only because he has never before made contact with a woman's feelings, but also because his own desires are so unrestrained. 'I am looking for someone who is completely at one with me,' Roderick says.

I have the impression that Roderick has taken his own fear of being constrained by dreary reality and projected it onto the woman of his dreams. He says that he wants this woman to be 'a strong, separate, individual character in her own right', and that he will provide servants to do the domestic tasks so that she will be 'free to be herself, with no constraints whatsoever in dealing with the fundamental, dreary facts of living'. But I suspect that Ailish is right when she says that the only way Roderick will start to overcome his fear of women is by hitching himself to someone who *is* willing to be his slave. 'I just don't think,' she says, 'that he is going to find the sort of person he needs,' whom she defines as a tolerant woman who keeps her thoughts to herself and insulates her husband from any children. Sometimes Ailish thinks that she should send Roderick off to the Philippines, where he might find a girl who would truly be his slave.

The mother of the Wild Man cannot be held responsible for his ferocity, and there is not much she can do to take the wildness out of him. What she can attempt, though, is to direct his feelings in a positive direction. When his insecurity reveals itself in megalomania, she can rein him in towards goals that are reasonable and more attainable. When his rage is expressed against her, she can try to recognise that he is more angry with the world than with her, and cajole him into articulating just what it is that he is feeling. As one mother said to me, whose Wild Son is now a marine, 'When he was threatening to kill me was probably the best time to talk to him. I don't believe in knocking my kids around, but I once picked him up and threw him onto a chair. I said "You are going to sit there and listen. You can scream your head off, but all I am trying to do is to understand. I can't understand when you are screaming at me. Tell me what you hate. Tell me what you dislike. Tell me what you feel." I punched a hole in him that way. From that point on, very slowly at first, he learned to recognise the way he was, to control it.'

Ultimately, the Wild Boy wants what every son seeks from his mother – for her to help him take control of his own life. The successful mother of a Wild Boy is the one who can fight his sense of insecurity and build up in him enough inner confidence to force him into recognising that he has her support even when, in another part of himself, he feels abandoned, discarded, without anybody upon whom he can lean. The general significance of this need for security will be explored more fully in the next chapter.

CHAPTER SIX

Inside the Triangle

'You have to tell the Oedipus story,' a friend remarked, expressing her surprise at having found no mention of the Greek hero in an earlier draft of this book.

'I am not sure it is relevant,' I replied, somewhat querulously.

'Don't be ridiculous! How can it not be relevant? How else do you think people understand the relationship between mothers, fathers and their sons?'

Maybe that was part of my problem. Although shocking in 1913, the Oedipus complex has become the banal theme tune of the psychoanalytic movement, whistled in homes throughout the world. For seven decades now, it has been the one aspect of Freudian thought that everybody felt they could grasp and talk about, thus rendering it progressively less clear, less interesting and less meaningful. 'By the time I arrived in Vienna,' wrote the author Elias Canetti of the early 1920s, 'the Oedipus complex had turned into a hackneyed prattle that no one failed to drone out; even the haughtiest scorner of mobs wasn't too good for an "Oedipus".'[1]

Acceptance of the basic Freudian idea is so widespread that autobiographies have been shaped around the notion that the subject wanted to murder his father so that he could make love to his mother. How could he have sought for anything else?

Such an attitude has also compelled intelligent men to spend years on analysts' couches, trawling through their unconscious minds in the expectation that they would eventually remember wanting to fuck mum and skewer dad. Failing to find evidence of such desires, they have sometimes concluded that everything Freud said must have been nonsense.

Is it time then to give up the Oedipus complex, to abandon the idea that boys feel a strong emotional and sexual pull towards their mothers, together with jealousy of their fathers, and that they must break from their mothers, ideally with help from dad, if they are to go off in search of other lovers? Not quite. Boys do experience feelings of great longing, jealousy and hatred towards their parents, and learn through them how to shape the pattern of their later desires, but there is no invariable pattern to these feelings.

The Sophocles play which inspired Freud's ideas says nothing at all about the desires which he describes. Oedipus has only friendly feelings for Polybus and Merope, the rulers of Corinth who had nursed him and brought him up as if they were his natural parents, which is why he leaves them in the hope of avoiding the outcome prophesied by the Delphic oracle. It is this attempt to evade his fate that actually leads to its fulfilment. Oedipus kills Laius not because he is his father, but because he is an arrogant and irritating stranger whom he meets at a cross-roads. He takes his place in Jocasta's bed, completely ignorant of the fact that this other stranger is his mother, because that is the prize awaiting whoever can solve the Sphinx's riddle. The source of horror to Sophocles was not so much a son's longing for his mother's body, not even the act of sex between a man and his biological mother, but the way that these actions can confuse all relationship categories, so that, by taking his mother to wife, Oedipus fathers children who are both daughters and half-sisters. As Canetti angrily observed, Freud's interpretation of Sophocles is somewhat simplistic: 'I knew who Oedipus was, I had read Sophocles, I refused to be deprived of the enormity of his fate.'[2]

Freud argued, though, that the play made such a powerful impact upon audiences because it reached down to a longing for his mother's body that every boy experiences. This is depicted as a pressing urge whose repression shapes a man's later psychic life. Murderous and lustful desires find expression, only to be blocked, becoming in the process more powerful than anything else which the boy might feel towards his parents. Oedipus does what every son, deep down, really wants to do. 'His destiny moves us only because it might have been ours – because the oracle laid the same curse on us before our birth as upon him. It was the fate of all of us, perhaps, to direct our first sexual impulse towards our mother and our first hatred and our first murderous wishes against our father. Our dreams convince us that this is so.'[3]

Every boy has his first experience of physical pleasure with his mother and most are free to make considerable use of her body. Many pubescent youths go on to report that mother featured in their first wet dreams, or became a focus of their early masturbation. This pair of facts has been taken as providing support for Freud's theory. But to conclude from this sort of evidence that every little boy formulates an urge to sleep with his mother as his father does, and that this urge is so powerful and pressing that it has to be pushed savagely underground, is a rather large jump of logic. 'Many a man,' says Jocasta in the play, 'has dreamt he found himself in bed with his mother. Once let fears like that upset you, life is intolerable.'[4]

The notion that the boy of three of four might see himself as being in competition with his father for mother's physical favours, because he longs to displace him in mother's bed and insert his penis inside her vagina, assumes that he makes some sort of connection between the physical affection he receives from mother and what goes on in the parental bedroom. It may be true that he normally wants from mother more than he can ever hope to receive, and that he is jealous of whoever else seems to be receiving the love for which he longs, but the idea that there is a firm shape to the boy's desire ignores the wildness that is inherent in the thought processes of little boys.

They may declare that they want to make babies with mum, but then they think and say a thousand other things which are really only distortions and half-understandings of the messages that they receive from their parents, conditional opinions emerging from a mush of feelings that will be discarded on the journey towards greater wisdom. An obsession with the Oedipus complex causes us to listen to only one part of what boys say to us, and to ignore all the rest, because we are encouraged to see the boy's longing for his mother as an overwhelming urge that only a father can disrupt.

The Oedipus complex retains such a hold upon the popular imagination because it acknowledges that family life is a site of continuous, in many ways very productive, tension between its members. Many fathers do feel excluded by the arrival of the child who competes for his partner's attention and would perhaps wish to emulate the actions of Laius when he bound his son's feet and had a shepherd dump him on the mountain side to die. And all children find themselves in competition with adults and siblings for love, attention, intimacy. Their failure to secure as much positive input as they would like arouses feelings of envy towards those who have, or who are imagined to have, more. And these emotions are the more powerful because they are rarely expressed. But exactly how and in what intensity they come to be deployed will be different in every context. The urges and attitudes described by Freud may sometimes seem important, but to portray them as part of a universal pattern is to overlook the variations in what happens between a mother, her son and his father.

The infant is from the start a player in the family's interpersonal dramas; his arrival changes the dynamic between family members, affecting the shape of each individual's longings and demands, and he in his turn will be affected by these shifts. Initially, though, he knows only that he has needs and that there are various people who apparently exist to satisfy them. He may find his mother more beneficent and more available, so that he prefers her, but there will be others who, because of their familiarity, will come to be accepted as alternatives. What the relationship may be between them, and how their availability to him might be determined, is not something to which he can be expected to give much thought.

Gradually, though, the little boy becomes aware that these people do not only exist to service him. They go to places where he does not and do things of which he has no grasp. He can become like them, because he too has the potential to evolve as a distinct person. He can relate to them in different ways, responding to the sounds they make, the smells they give off, the way they make him feel, just as they relate to each other. Dimly, too, he comes to understand that the relationships which these people have with each other have some sort of impact upon the way he is treated.

The boy becomes used to the parenting situation in which he finds himself. He may come to recognise that one parent is there a lot, another occasionally. This he can accept. But if one of these two disappears, he will feel that the walls within which he operates have been torn down. Just the prospect of them breaking up may come to stir real terror. If his parents live happily together, he will not have much cause to worry about them. Intense anxiety can be stirred, though, if he experiences signs of tension, witnessing blows being exchanged in the sitting room, or pans of baked beans flung angrily across the kitchen table. He may lie in bed at night, hear them rowing and wonder what the implications of all this ruckus might be for him. He may be aware that they sometimes drink a lot and then behave in ways that seem rather strange and out of character. He will not know what to make of all these impressions, but he may well feel that in some indefinable way his security is threatened.

Simon, the hospital consultant whose emulation of his

mother's money-management skills was described in Chapter Four, has mostly happy memories of his childhood. However, one disturbing occurrence made a deep impression. He was four and his parents had just had a major row. His mother picked up her baby girl, took Simon by the hand and marched him up the road. This party of three then sat under a tree for half an hour as a storm began to blow, giving Simon the clear impression that they had left home and were never going back. 'Life,' he recalls some forty years later, 'was suddenly not as secure as it seemed.' Simon's drive to build up wealth so that he can give his parents a comfortable standard of living may have been motivated by this experience. Through it, he expresses his need to keep them together, so that they will still be there for him.

While the source of what appears to be driving the boy's parents apart is likely to be a mystery, an even greater one is the force that holds them together; the secret of the bedroom, the special nature of their union. Whether he sees them being intimate together, or experiences them as cold towards each other, he will become dimly conscious of the fact that they retreat to a double bed at night, maybe sometimes also on a Sunday afternoon, and that something happens there between them. The arrival of siblings, or his own questions about how he came into being, will make him aware that this activity too has something to do with his existence. The boy's endless questions concerning the process of reproduction reflect the extent of his need to know about this. 'Where is your borning place?' Ted repeatedly asked his mother when he was five. On one occasion, as he recalls, she pulled her knickers down, pointed to her genital area and said 'It is there', which left him little better informed.

The boy has to deal with many other mysteries that take a great deal of unpicking. What is his penis for? What does it mean that his father has one and his mother does not? How does what his parents do together in bed relate to their ability to satisfy the needs that he has of them? And what part is he going to play in the power struggle between his parents? His life between the 'oedipal' discovery of his parents' relationship and the beginnings of his own adolescence, is a continuous exploration of these questions.

Whatever the particulars of the boy's situation, whether he has one female carer or several, one father or a host of stepfathers, he will pick up information from many sources about how he might behave towards other people. He will then try to use the repertoire of emotional responses that he has acquired to deal with the pressures that are placed upon him, and to secure what he wants from others. It is because, in the traditional household, a mother's love is so much more available than a father's that it often makes sense for the boy to declare at first a greater allegiance to her. He has more opportunity, anyway, to see how she operates, and to hear her point of view. Thus it was that Kevin, for example, came to view his parents' marriage very much from his mother's perspective. If he saw her cry, he would give her a hug. If things seemed to be going badly, he would suggest that a divorce might be the better option. 'I was turned against my father,' he recalls. 'Because I saw her side of it, I felt he was a bit of a bastard.'

Spending hour after hour with her boy, often feeling quite resentful at the lack of attention she receives from her husband, many a mother makes a conscious effort to win over her son. 'I am aware,' says Yvonne, 'of having a special relationship with him and of sometimes consciously excluding my husband. I want to be the better one of the two parents. I want to be the one.' She does not hesitate to reveal to Joe just what it is about her husband that drives her crazy, and she does not feel that it is her responsibility to mitigate the jealousy that the father feels when witnessing the special relationship between mother and son. 'I cannot do it for him,' she says.

Karen's husband walked out when her second son was only two. His subsequent contact with the boys has been confined to flying in occasionally from South Africa and showering them with presents. Karen has never hesitated to let them know exactly what she feels about such behaviour. 'I think,' she says, 'he has let them down so badly that he does not deserve anything from them. It scares me shitless that they will resume a relationship with him. I really don't want it. It would devalue everything I have done in the last sixteen years.'

Robert Bly, the men's movement guru, argues that if a son sees his father as somewhat tarnished, it is the result of some sort of 'conspiracy' between a mother and her son. 'The son,' he writes, 'often grows up with a wounded image of his father – not brought about necessarily by the father's actions, or words, but based on the mother's observation of these words or actions.'[5] What this amounts to is a demand that the mother should cover for her husband and report that he is wonderful even if he clearly is not. In reality, if the son takes on board his mother's negativity about father, that is usually because the man himself has not established a deep emotional bond to his child. Children watch their parents all the time, and draw their own conclusions from what they see, without necessarily needing to adopt a mother's interpretation.

Over time, indeed, a mother's criticisms will often have the effect of turning a son against *her*. As long as the relationship he has with his mother provides the emotional basis for his life, the denigration of father will not be something a son wants to challenge. But a time will come when the strength of his desire to loosen those ties, and to seek attachments elsewhere, may cause him to hear his mother's words in a different way. For is he not a male like his father? Does he not live in a relationship with his mother, as his father did or does? What reason then is there to think that he too will not become an object of abuse and denigration? What was his mother's role in his father's absence or collapse? What does she plan to do with *him*?

The son who for years has taken his mother's side may then leap to his father's defence. The very fact that dad has been so much absent from his life may make it all the easier to idealise him. Henry, for example, had accepted for years that the rows between his parents which led to their separation had been due to his father's mental illness. But a deterioration in the relationship he had with his mother forced him to ask why a man who had seemed okay for so long should begin to behave in an impossible fashion. Why, he asked his mother, did it happen that way? The answers she gave never satisfied him. In such a case, the boy may come to see himself in the man he has learned to mock; his initial suspicion of mother's attitude turns into a burning resentment; the loving son becomes a raging fury.

It is easy at this stage for the son to forget everything that his mother once did for him, and all the anger that he used to feel against his father. When I first started the research for this book, I blamed my mother for nearly every aspect of myself that I did not like. But then I came across a letter that I had written when I was nine, in which I asked my father why he was never there to help me with my homework or with other problems. 'Are you really my father?' I wrote. 'Whenever I need you, you're not there. When you're there, what a bad temper! I think you might have killed me.' Reading the letter released many memories of occasions when I had longed for him to come and rescue me from what I saw as my mother's irrational oppression or emotional demands, and he had either failed to arrive or refused to play the role that I wished him to when he came. I threw the anger onto my mother because I had given up hope that my father would ever come to my rescue. He never did.

The son seems to move from needing his mother to wanting a demonstration from his father of how he can become a 'man'. Having once been close to the mother who loved him and supported him, he turns away from her and looks for the satisfactions to be found elsewhere. Insofar as his mother constrains him, or expresses a negative view of his father, he turns against her. The son may now want to kill his mother and seek his father's assistance in doing so. 'Because I was powerless to break free of the stranglehold,' recalls broadcaster and writer Ludovic Kennedy in his autobiography, 'my feelings towards her grew from acute discomfort in her presence to active hatred. I hated her so much and so continuously I used to pray for her death – though had she died all of a sudden, I shudder to think of the burden of guilt I would have borne. Once, in desperation, I tried to enlist the support of my father when she mildly rebuked me for something I had said to her. "Don't you understand," I said to him, almost in tears, "I hate her. I really hate her."'[6]

The aiming of these particular brickbats at mother is not an inevitable part of male development, but the consequence of traditional parenting practice. The boy rails against his mother because she is the one whom he must hate if he is to establish his autonomy and independence. She has provided the parameters to his life so far, and he begins to chafe under the restraints she imposes. It is not someone 'male' that he sees in his father so much as someone who is 'other' to the person from which he must now try to escape.

The issue for the boy is how he can move on. What the son on the edge of adolescence is really looking for is recognition from both his parents that he is ready to take this step. He feels encouraged if his father talks to him, shows him things and treats him like the grown-up person he feels himself to be. He likes it if his mother responds a little as she does to a lover when he cuddles up to her and kisses her on the cheek. He is not just seeking warmth and security as he did before, but playing a little with desire. He may recount his deeds in a way that is designed to impress her, or tell her outrageous things in the hope of making her laugh. He is trying out his seductive charms, testing his powers and preparing his next move.

The dramas of this stage in life are generally taken to be further evidence of the boy's forbidden longing to displace his father in the marital bed. But his behaviour has as much to do with a desire to break free as with any longing to come close: this is really only the final stage of the boy's growth under his mother's tutelage. 'When a child experiences incestuous feelings or fantasies,' remarks psychotherapist Andrew Samuels, 'he can be seen as unconsciously attempting to add enriching layers of experience to his personality by his contact with the parent.'[7] The drama of desire that takes place between a mother and her son is not so much an attempt to stick close to his mother, rather a recognition of the struggle that is involved in drawing apart.

As the mother becomes aware that her son is now a fully-fledged individual, and that separation looms as a real prospect, she may feel a special wave of affection towards him. She may be inspired to take a particular pleasure in feeding him his favourite dish or in buying him clothes. She will listen to him more intently and laugh much louder at his jokes. Part of her wants to keep him by her side, part of her wants to enjoy him to the full while she still has him there, part of her too may want to encourage his romantic skills. For whatever reason, it may seem to her partner or to her other children that she has a 'thing' about her pubescent son. But at the same time she may find herself looking forward to the day when he has moved away, set up his own house and started a family.

The last thing the boy really wants at this stage is to be trapped with his mother. He craves freedom to go off and to make his own life. He seeks from his mother and his father encouragement to do just that. This is why he wants them to respond to his attempts at seduction, with a flutter of the eyelids in his mother's case, with an angry outburst from his father. To assume that the boy really wishes to usurp his father is to argue that staying put appears more desirable than journeying on. Moving away and seeking love from someone else is an awesome undertaking, one whose every move has to be endlessly rehearsed and thought about. If either parent forgets that their boy is working his passage away from them, his hopes are betrayed.

The common assumption that a mother wants her son to stay beside her forever, and that the boy is too weak to break away on his own, creates a role for the father as someone who must intervene so as to break the bonds that hold the boy fast to his mother. Following the logic of this sort of argument, some suggest that the father's most essential job is to step in only when the boy is on the edge of adolescence, take him in hand and give him directions down the High Road to masculinity. 'Women can change the embryo to a boy, but only men can change the boy to a man,' Robert Bly argues.[8] This process is best achieved, Bly's view sometimes seems to be, if a father takes his son on a trip to the forest, where they can fish together, frolic and run with the deer.

Bly gives the father a very limited role and one which almost justifies his keeping a distance from family life in the early stages of his child's life so that he can be a more effective agent of 'separation' later on. A mother's love is seen as a murky, suspicious and dangerous force, potentially responsible for all the bad things that boys can get up to. Father stands aloof from this mêlée, able to say of any emotional misfortune which befalls his children that it is not his fault. The only failing he can have is not being around at the appropriate time to snip the links between mother and son.

But the father who only becomes interested in his son when he is old enough to go fishing for pike or willing to be jostled in the crowd at a football match can never hope to establish a meaningful relationship with him. How much, after all, can two males learn from each other when sitting quietly by a river? As psychotherapist Heather Formaini, author of *Men: The Darker Continent*[9], observes, 'When you fish you have to be silent. How does he find out about his father? How does he work out what it is to be a man? It must be desperately confusing. There is nothing that little girls do which requires absolute silence.' Many a boy has been mesmerised by the experience of being taken in hand by the good-looking chap who until then had not done much more than walk through the door and say 'Hello', and may even describe such an experience as 'great' – but that does not mean it counts as satisfactory parenting.

There is no one stage at which a boy starts to require his father's serious attention. He needs someone to turn to whenever things become stormy between himself and his mother, when he is confused by a friend's reactions, has trouble with work or friends or just wants someone to talk to about life, his future, his hopes and dreams. All too often, though, father is of no help: he has abdicated responsibility to mother or does not care. When Ludovic Kennedy called upon his father for assistance, the man just looked at his feet and said nothing.

Ideally, the son who feels constricted and frustrated in his relationship to mother would be helped by his father to modulate his response. If he felt burdened by his mother's neediness, his father could let him know that someone else was willing to take a share of the load. Through giving him insight into his own experience of mother, the father would help his son to understand his feelings better and deal with them more effectively. With his father's support, he could more easily make the transition from childish connection to mature attachment.

The boy needs to hear someone else articulating the sort of negative feelings he necessarily has towards his 'bad' mother. Otherwise, he cannot easily come to believe that it is possible for him to express whatever anger he has against her: he may fear that, if he did, he would destroy the relationship. He will experience his mother as needing him, but fail to develop a sense that it might be possible for him to sustain his relationship with her and also become an autonomous individual. 'Being able to observe relationships that take place between other people,' says psychotherapist Paul van Heeswyck, 'helps one imagine oneself from someone else's point of view. It helps one learn to be an outsider, rather than just being involved in something. If you don't get this, you are always dancing to somebody else's tune. You are their captive and their slave.'

The son who grows up without any experience of his parents enjoying each other while relating to him as well will later find it difficult to experience the arrival of his own child with a feeling of joy, seeing him or her instead as a threat to his relationship with the mother. He may respond by leaving or by launching a flood of criticism at his wife, thus bringing his fears to fulfilment as effectively as Oedipus did by seeking to evade the oracle's prediction. Unless something forces him to think quite seriously about how he has been influenced by his early experiences, he will not find it easy to become for his own child the parent that his own father could never be to him. It took Milos some fifteen years to tell Jana that the birth of their first son had made him feel that he was unnecessary to her. 'You could not have been further from the truth,' she replied. 'I never needed you more than I did then.'

The boy who receives the influence of only one parent can learn everything he needs to know about being intimate and quite a lot about being separate, but he cannot acquire the confidence he needs to confront the feelings that he has about either parent. He will not find it easy to break from his mother, or to form a strong relationship with another. The plight of the Lover Sons, who suffer most severely from this problem, is the subject of the next chapter.

CHAPTER SEVEN

Lover Sons

'I was born hating my father,' wrote D. H. Lawrence with reference to his novel *Sons and Lovers*. 'This has been a kind of bond between me and my mother. We have loved each other, almost with a husband and wife love.'[1] The book depicts a son whose mother nourishes his intellectual and spiritual development while sapping his capacity for independence. 'These sons,' Lawrence wrote in an earlier letter, 'are urged into life by their reciprocal love of their mother – urged on and on. But when they come to manhood, they can't love, because their mother is the strongest power in their lives, and holds them.'[2]

The fathers of such sons are no use to them at all. Lawrence's novel presents a lurid vision of the kind of man who remains absent from his children's lives, even though he does come home at night and sit down with them at the kitchen table. It is not just that the slosh of ale all too often puts him in a foul mood; his emotional limitations render him incapable of understanding or forming a relationship to his young. In one of the book's most poignant scenes, Walter Morel returns from work, hears that his wife has just given birth and demands dinner before going upstairs to have a look. He is not much more involved when he reaches the bedside. 'He stood at a loss what to say next. He was tired, and this bother was rather a nuisance to him, and he didn't quite know where he was.

'"A lad, tha' says," he stammered.'[3]

It is some time since Lawrence wrote his book, and the sort of mining community that he described has mostly been destroyed, but there are still many fathers who offer no help at all in bringing up their children. In such circumstances, it is not surprising that some women (among them, many of the Demanding Mothers from Chapter One) have come to feel that they are better off rearing children without the bother of having to deal with the men who released their semen inside them. Jill, for example, had her first two kids with men whom she had no intention of marrying, and she argues that her son benefited from this. 'He was brought up without any sort of strain. That lack of conflict gives a kid a heck of a chance. It makes them very stable. I hate children being in conflict. I hate them having undertones in their lives. It is awful, because they are so very sensitive.'

I went to interview Jill in order to discover why her elder son Vincent, a computer technician now in his late twenties, still lives at home with mother, and she immediately impressed me as a forceful personality. 'Withdraw', the first word I heard from her, was directed at two Dobermans who bayed at me from behind a glass front door. She hastened to reassure me that they had already eaten their dinner, so that I need not be afraid. Tall and thin, with her hair dyed ginger, Jill ushered me into the hall and then went ahead to make sure there were no dead cats or birds lying on the carpet. She treated me as a man in recovery from some horrid trauma, who had to be protected from any sort of further shock. I was not surprised to learn that Jill takes children out on assault courses into the Welsh hills.

Everything that Jill has to say about men reveals deep scorn. As a girl, she was disappointed that her father would not take a stand against his nagging wife. She used to wish that he would hit her, or use the pistol that he kept upstairs, but he never did. In her capacity as commander of the local cadet squadron, Jill reports that she constantly has to deal with inadequate men who are being pushed forward by their powerful wives. And contempt hardly describes the feelings that she has towards the husband she acquired when Vincent was six, a man who was 'awkward, argumentative and down-right ignorant'. Altogether, she finds in the irresponsibility of men their only virtue. 'I have often thought,' she says, 'that if we went right back to nature, it would be much better. Male dog does his bit and goes. Women are the stronger species and they know it.'

Despite having such a low view of adult men, perhaps because she had such a low view of other males, Jill desperately wanted a boy to shape and to love. The years that followed the birth of her second child, a daughter, were tough. With half her income going on childminders, she had very little left with which to feed her children and herself. Her iron level was low and she was seriously malnourished. Exhausted, she eventually put both her children up for adoption. But when the time came, it was only the girl that she could bear to let go. 'Vincent,' she says, 'was the one person who loved me for being me.'

Jill wanted a male who would love her, and who would be worth loving in return because he would become the man of her dreams. She would protect him from the influence of all the male weaklings and nincompoops around, so that he might become someone who would stand by her in his turn. Vincent has always risen to that challenge. At the age of five, Jill recalls, he shut a door against his shrieking, hysterical grandmother who had been chasing her. A few years later, when she married the Welshman with a horrid temper, it was Vincent who, by throwing a cup of boiling water over his genitals, not only secured his mother's release from a violent attack, but also drove the man out of the house for good. And when his stepfather's in-laws responded by launching a campaign to try and drive her from the town – by prowling around the house at night and driving cars towards her – Vincent stood by her side as protector and emotional prop.

Jill welcomes the alliance that Vincent offers, but in reality she does most of the work for herself. When she calls upon him to aid her, whether to expel a violent husband, fill the space of a departed man, or simply help out against bailiffs, social workers and intrusive neighbours, she never puts pressure upon him to do more than he is capable of, never creates a situation in which he might feel inadequate. 'You are my little man,' she tells him, and he is gratified enough by the warmth with which she speaks to embrace that role. But some of the emphasis is on the 'little', because Jill still wants to prove that she is stronger than any man, can do without a man, even while she clings close to her own son.

Perhaps it is only that she wants a man who will serve her. Jill sees it as another virtue in her model of single parenthood that Vincent learned so early to help her with domestic tasks. 'If there had been a man around,' she says, 'he wouldn't have had to chop wood or mend windows.' He quickly learned to cook, clean and assist with household maintenance. He was good at repairing electronic items. And when he came home with his first wage packet, he offered his mother all the cash. 'I had Vincent's support all along,' she recalls. 'He contributed many times in many ways. He recognised that we were a family, and that our survival was very dependent on each other.'

Vincent argues that he stays at home with his mother only because it made sense to do so in an area where wages are low and housing relatively expensive. I was at first disposed to accept this argument. Later, though, it came to seem more likely that it was his mother's love that held him. A few days after we had first met, I ran into Vincent's mother at a railway station. Whereas she had seemed a little frumpish before, she was now dressed up, showing off her shapely long legs under a short green coat. When my companion complimented her on the way her hair had been done, she revealed that it was Vincent's work. Where was she off to? To meet up with her son and do some shopping. I concluded that, for want of a satisfactory husband, Jill had made Vincent into something better, the sort of man who cuts a woman's hair and takes her to the shops.

Cyril is an older version of Vincent. Neither he nor his mother had ever seen much of his father, who would go away to sea for two-year stretches with the merchant navy. But Cyril nevertheless felt enormously sad for mother when his father announced that in future he would be spending his months of leave with another, more sexually compliant, woman. (Cyril's mother had decided that the best way to avoid having any more babies was to abstain completely from sex.) 'I felt,' he says, 'that my mother did not appear to be the capable type who could look after herself. She seemed rather vulnerable emotionally. It made me feel a little bit as if I wanted to look after her.' At first, this only entailed doing more around the house than either his brother or sister, as well as trying to provide emotional support. Eventually though, he decided to set up house for her so that they could live together, which they did until the day she died.

The love that keeps the Lover Sons at home, or causes them to return there after a brief and abortive attempt to get on in the outside world, is not something slight and insubstantial. Vincent speaks with passion of the admiration he feels for his mother and how he wants to be like her. 'Both of us,' he says, 'are very caring, very tolerant and very patient, but we are also tough.' The Lover Son does not hang around just so that he can eat her shepherd's pie and have his shirts ironed: he also wants to help out and provide support. He stays with mother because he respects and esteems her, because he has a good relationship with her, and because he recognises that, with his father either physically gone or emotionally absent, she has nobody else to take care of her.

He may give the impression that he is making an attempt to break away from mother and establish himself in a relationship to another woman, but he will never apply himself to the task with any great enthusiasm. A degree of inertia hangs around his mating efforts, either because he is frightened of what would happen if a woman were to come too close, or because he feels that the relationship with mother is too precious to be put at risk, even though, sexually, it is incomplete.

Vincent says that he quite likes the idea of being married, but quickly adds that he would also be content if it never happened. He has had girlfriends, but the description he offers of his relationships with them lacks any indication of serious commitment. He reports with pride that none of these liaisons ever went sour; the two of them just drifted apart. 'I like it easy-going,' he reports. 'I don't like being put under pressure.' He also says that one of the reasons he is generally unimpressed by the girls he meets is because they do not really rate beside his mother. 'I would not want a wimp for a wife,' he says. 'I need someone with bottle and personality.' Why, he implies, should he want a relationship with someone else when the one he has at the moment is so satisfying?

Still a virgin, although now in his early seventies, Cyril speaks with rather less equanimity about his failure to find someone he could marry. He blames his mother for having given him the impression that she did not want him to mix with girls. Whether because of her distaste for sex, or because she was frightened of losing her younger son, she told him that girls would not be welcome in the house and should not be discussed. He put off casual sexual encounters, telling himself that he would eventually find one that would be 'meaningful' enough to justify going up against his mother, but in the event he has never gone close to any woman apart from her.

Another reason for Cyril's celibacy was that he operated

on the principle that he would marry the first woman who presented no challenge and put no obstacles in his way. As soon as there was any hint that the process of wooing might stir up difficult emotions or result in any sort of tension, he fled. The girls he met struck him as intrusive and probing, intent on finding out things about him that he did not wish to reveal, seeking to peer behind his mask. 'They were,' he says of the young women he took to the cinema when he was in his late teens, 'always asking me questions about my personal feelings.' He did once feel that there might be a possibility of some progress towards romance when he became attracted to a girl he met at work whose simple style of dress and direct, friendly manner seemed not to threaten him with any sort of exposure, but when another man appeared on the scene, he promptly withdrew from the contest.

Having never had to negotiate with his father for access to his mother, Cyril has not learned to deal with romantic rivalry, and the fear of being humiliated. He was so afraid of being shown up by another man that he decided it was safer for him to remain with his mother: she was the least dangerous option because she never provoked him, challenged him or threatened to reveal his weaker side. He felt safe, and gradually more so as her deterioration into wordless debility removed any threat that his relationship to her had aroused. Cyril says of his mother's later years, when a stroke had made her largely dependent upon his care, that they were the happiest he has ever enjoyed.

One might suppose that Cyril had reached an age when hope would be pretty much behind him. There is, though, a widow who is keen to form a relationship with him now that he is free from the burden of looking after mother. And yet, even when offered a last chance to experience a real union, something still holds him back. 'She is so different in many ways,' he says mysteriously in answer to my question about what this might be. 'I don't think it is anything I can quite put my finger on.' After I press him to say a little more, he recalls that, even fifty years previously, when he first knew the woman, she was not the sort of person he would want to marry. Why was that? 'She was popular with the men, if you know what I mean,' he finally declared. Cyril is so much in awe of females that he cannot risk going with a woman who once caught the eye of other men, even though his rivals have been cremated or now dribble into their beards.

When I first started thinking about these Lover Sons, I was disposed to defend them against the mockery to which they are so often exposed, and argue against the assertion that, because they eat with mum, go shopping with mum, massage her feet, cut her hair, and empty her commode when she becomes incontinent, they are not really 'men' at all. I considered that there was something admirable about the way in which, instead of anxiously trying to throw off the chains that bind them to mother, they take on the responsibility of providing her with dutiful care. It seemed to me that the relationships they had with their mothers were much warmer than those between many men and their wives. And it was certainly true that they had never done any woman serious harm, unlike those who are violent or commit other acts of cruelty against their partners. Could one not argue that, by departing so far from our stereotypes of what it means to be a man, these Lovers Sons had something to teach all men?

I could find nobody who agreed even a little with this point of view. Most argued that becoming a mature adult necessarily involved leaving mother and taking up with someone else. 'If you have a wife you beat up,' remarked therapist Jonathan Courage 'at least there is some damage you can deal with. But if you stop dead and fester in an old relationship, you can't deal with it, you can only move out of it.' I think this attitude underestimates the extent to which these Lover Sons do develop within their relationships with mum, so that they come to take genuine pleasure in doing things for her, rather than just adopting the take-take-take mode that is characteristic of so many mother-son relationships. But I also agree that there is something which these men are repressing, and this comes across in the apparent idealisation of their mothers. It is because they were never given any sort of encouragement to express negative feelings about their mothers that they stay put, trapped in the maternal cocoon.

The situation with their mothers may have been so gratifying for these men that they never did feel angry with her, as other sons do, for failing to give them a completely satisfactory experience in childhood, and perhaps as a result they never did long for something better and more complete. Perhaps the mother's determination to hold on to him enabled her to offer him a loving intimacy that was more than simply 'good enough', so that it was impossible for him to give her up. But perhaps too these Lover Sons simply opted for the easy option because anything else just seemed too frightening. They constructed personalities that were built around denial and cowardice. The easy-going natures to which both of them confessed, reflected an absolute refusal to express their feelings. 'I am one of those people,' Cyril says, 'who tend to accept things and make the best of it.'

It is because he has never tried to re-negotiate his relationship with mother, and to tackle the things about it which do not satisfy him, that he is so afraid of attempting a relationship with anyone else. With mother he feels safe, but then she does not ask of him, as a lover would, that he be fully intimate with her: she knows that to do this would be to destroy the understanding which they have. Mother and son live together, but they never face the deficiencies in their relationship. As a result, the Lover Son cannot learn to negotiate the perils of intimacy, and to recognise that it is possible to be dependent upon another woman without suffocating in her embrace.

The next chapter looks at how other sons do manage to break free from mother's embrace and start to form a life that is independent of hers.

CHAPTER EIGHT

Breaking Away

Adolescent boys tend to terrify not only their mothers but almost everyone else. In popular imagination, they are brutish, uncivilised and untameable. They do not wash; their vocabulary is limited to twenty words, all rude ones; they sniff glue and they never answer any questions. They drop litter; kick tin cans across streets and run off with traffic cones. They hang around in gangs, steal cars, frighten old ladies, make girls pregnant because they will not use condoms and never accept responsibility for anything that they do.

Although the reality is usually somewhat less frightening than this, alarming things do happen to boys (and girls) when they reach their teens. The rows that ensue can leave a mother wondering just how it was that her happy, cheerful, loving boy could have turned into such a monster. Edna O'Brien vividly captures a mother's response to this sort of situation in her novel *Time and Tide*, where she recounts a dead-of-night confrontation between the heroine and her elder son: 'A catalogue of grievances on both sides were aired, and even as she heard them or voiced them, she thought how muddled it all was, how far removed from the nub of the matter, which was that the love they once had, the sweet vital reserves of love, had vanished, disappeared like those streams that go underground without leaving a trace.'[1]

What the son seeks from his mother in adolescence is not so different from what he wanted before. He still needs her close to make him feel safe, and yet he also requires her to be as far away as possible so that he can assert his independence. 'It's a question,' says psychotherapist Paul van Heeswyck, 'of trying to get the distance right.' What changes is the boy's definition of the appropriate distance. He wants his mother ever further away from him so that he can try out his wings and learn to fly, and yet he also needs her to be there when he comes in to land. His rebellions are no longer simply tests of his power, they are assertions of his separate identity. Everything he does is designed in some way to prepare for the day when he will break completely free. And yet the situation is never clear-cut; for while he asserts autonomy in the morning, he may still want cuddles in the afternoon. Since the boy feels abandoned if she goes too far away, and yet stifled if she comes too close, it is quite impossible for any mother to get the distance right. 'In order to make sure that they are what they want to be,' wrote psychoanalyst Bruno Bettelheim about adolescents, 'to some degree they try to be also what their parents do not want them to be, on the presumption that this alone can assure them of their independence. It is this ambivalent and often contradictory wish that makes the life of the adolescent so torn and difficult, and also what makes living with him so problematic for his parents.'[2]

Previously the boy's greatest fear was mother's disappearance, now it is that she will block his passage. He may talk about obstructions being placed in front of him in a way that appears quite paranoid: the weaknesses that stop him reaching his goals are his own, and yet he blames his mother for them. She, hearing the rejection in his manner towards her, prickling against his rebukes, recognising too that he is, or ought to be, almost mature and rational now, no longer feels so inclined to carry his anger, to let it simply bounce off her. She wants recognition from him for what she has done, and that is something which he is extremely reluctant to give.

The tensions between a mother and her son are not just the consequence of a necessary disentangling, a breaking of bonds; they reflect a growing gap between the boy's fantasies and his mother's anxieties. He wants to believe that he is now all-powerful and can do anything. She recognises his limitations and worries that, unless he sees them too, he will end up in serious trouble. The result is that she seems intent only on knocking him down. He insists against all the evidence that everything is possible for him, that he has the strength to free himself from his need of mother. He wants to be unfettered, to go everywhere and to taste all the richness from which he feels that he has been excluded for too long. And yet he is stuck in the family home with his apparently conservative and cautious parents.

Much of what he does to prove that he is in control of his own life only provokes his mother into further attempts to lay down the law. The mess in his bedroom suggests that he is quite incapable of looking after himself. His inability to utter anything other than monosyllables is all the evidence she needs to become convinced that he has absolutely no social skills. His refusal to do his homework clearly indicates that he is going to end his days as a street-cleaner. And when he comes down to breakfast at midday with his pupils still enlarged by whatever he was smoking or swallowing the night before, even that seems an unattainable goal; for he is destined to die in the gutter or on the floor of some bleak, crumbling apartment in a desolate neighbourhood.

His outlook causes repeated clashes with his mother. It is because she cares for him that she has to remind him he is not yet mature. She worries about his future, wants him to have a good start in life and tries to prevent him messing up his chances. She longs for him to be strong, capable and independent, but not enough of these qualities are evident in the hunk who lumbers around her kitchen, asking for the whereabouts of a clean shirt or his dinner, to give her any confidence that he will reach that position without her help, which means challenging him, reproaching him and bullying him. And part of her fervour, her persistence, comes from the fact that it is not just his future that is at stake, but the final judgement upon her performance as a mother. 'I am the failure if he does not pass his exams,' says Karen of her elder boy. 'I am trying to prove that I can bring up two kids who will succeed in life.'

A mother feels too that this is her last chance to influence her son into realising the dreams she had when he was born. In reality, it is almost certainly too late, but when he says that he is bored and fed up, she may try once more to make him interested in the music that she likes or the books that she once enjoyed. But he is not likely to listen to his mother now, and anyway he prefers to spend all day in front of a computer. How then can she celebrate her son who does nothing with which she can identify, who spends so much time loafing around with his friends or playing football? 'It doesn't make me proud,' says Yvonne of her son Joe's sporting prowess. 'I don't care. I should care. I admire him. I think he is handsome. I like looking at his legs. But I find all this hopping about incredibly tedious. It is the side of men that I find ridiculous.'

Every remark that a mother makes about her son's immaturity, clumsiness or irresponsibility leaves him feeling small, convinced that to his mother he will never be anything other than her little baby, so that perhaps he can never be anything else to anybody at all. By still trying to tell him how to live his life, what he ought to be doing that he so adamantly refuses, mother seems to deny her son the respect for which he longs. He wants her to see that he has turned out well, that he has become a man, that he is strong, resolute and capable, someone she can rely upon and trust, and yet all she does is scream at him. When she does that, refusing to let him know that she believes in him, he will do those things that make her mad.

The fact that her remarks hurt so much is testimony to the value he still places upon her concern and care. That is one reason why he must shout at her and repudiate the view that she seems to have of him. He will also be fighting off his nostalgia for those earlier days when things between them seemed much easier, when he could accept his mother's abundant love and support because he did not feel threatened by it. The boy's quest for independence is often so stormy because the forces that call him back to where he came from, to helpless dependency and enslavement, are powerful too.

And so they fight and bicker, because their views of his behaviour are so far apart. Every attempt she makes to shape him fosters another passionate assertion of his autonomy. 'You were so nice when you were small,' she may say to him unhelpfully, 'and now you are so mean.' Many a mother gives up at this point, because she does not want to be so hard, to make herself into an object of reproach and recrimination. If a father is available, she may surrender her old responsibilities to him. It is his job now to discipline her son, she will say. He must tell him to work harder, dress more tidily, do some chores around the house and turn the music down. She cannot cope anymore, and he is a male after all. He is the one who will have to get angry and provoke the stand-up rows. She will then step in as the gentle, loving mother, even though the feelings that her partner expresses are hers as well.

There is no way of evading at least some of this awful rancour: the son needs to discover what he feels about his mother and about himself, so as to learn ways to deal with his negative feelings. If it does not happen now, it will have to happen later, or never happen at all, which would be worse. Were he to have his oft-stated wish fulfilled and find himself living away from home before he has prepared the way himself, he would know even less than most adult men do about how to form a relationship, how to live with other people. He stays, then, as long as he needs – or as long as he can endure. The paradox for mother is that her son continuously denies he has any need of her, but at the same time he calls repeatedly for her help, support and assistance. He asks her for recognition, money and love, while denying that he has any obligations to fulfil. His fantasies of independence are sharply out of tune with reality.

Her responses leave him feeling confused. What is it that she wants of him? If she would like him to be independent, why will she not let him go hitchhiking around Europe with his loutish schoolmates? If she wants him eventually to be married, why can he not go and look for a girlfriend at the disco on Thursday night? She seems not to trust him, and yet she speaks of having great hopes for him. 'In some ways,' says Joe, 'she wants me to act like a grown-up. In some ways she thinks I am quite small. She still wants to take care of me. Sometimes I am not too sure what she really wants. Just to keep an eye on me perhaps.'

When Fidel was in his mid-teens, he started to complain that his mother would not permit him to explore where he wanted to go in life. Birgit could not understand this at all. She had always backed him in his enthusiasms, whether for sport, study or music, and she could not remember ever stopping him from doing anything. What irritated him, though, was that she seemed to place so much more importance on academic work, which he found hard, and never took a really serious interest in his athletics, where it was much easier for him to excel.

Interpreting this as an attempt by his mother to block him, Fidel expressed his anger by abandoning both his books *and* his running shoes. He started to steal money from her purse; he was caught shoplifting in a London record store and he then joined up with a group of boys who sprayed graffiti on underground trains. Birgit became accustomed to coming back from work to a house that reeked of drinkers' vomit. On one occasion, she found that her son's bed had been packed out with pillows, a sure sign that he had gone down to the train depot for a midnight frenzy with a spray can. The next day, she sat down at the kitchen table to talk. 'He told me to back off,' Birgit recalls. 'He would live his life no matter what I did.'

Birgit was relieved and excited to discover that her son wanted to relieve her of the worries she had about him. 'It sort of let me off a bit,' she says. 'I had always found the responsibility very difficult to handle.' But four years later, Birgit feels that her son has failed to live up to the promise implied in that conversation. He still complains about her reluctance to let him go and to loosen her power over him; she still feels frustrated at his inability to establish his financial independence, arguing that if she is going to keep on bailing him out, she should have some say in how he runs his life. 'I don't think I want to hold him,' she says. 'I like independence around me because it gives me freedom. I resent him saying he wants to be independent and then being dependent.'

The tensions between Fidel and Birgit partly involve a quarrel between two cultures, between a mother who was brought up in Germany after the Second World War, and a son who was born into welfare-state Britain, between a young man who believes that he will never starve because there will always be someone to pull him out of the gutter, and a mother who worries that her son does not have the wherewithal to survive without her, and who also wishes that he would get off her back. But theirs is also the argument that goes on in many households between a son who wants to believe that he is completely autonomous and a mother who knows that he is not, and who does not accept that she should play along with his fantasy that he is independent.

The process of separation between Fidel and Birgit derived some of its intensity from the fact that he was an only child and she a single mother. Their isolation heightened her sense of responsibility for him and his fear of being forever entangled with her. Karen, another single mother, had an even more difficult time with her elder son. Intense rows became the only way they could find to shake off the closeness they once had. When I went to see her, the conflict between them had just about become unbearable. 'I know it is going to be one hell of a wrench,' she said. 'It is going to leave a hole in my life. But for both our sakes he has got to go. I never thought I would get to the point where I don't want this conflict around anymore, but I actually want him to leave home.'

Some mothers, frightened by the implications of their sons' new assertiveness, try to stop the process of change, and in consequence make things even worse. 'The longer the mother believes in her oneness with her son,' psychoanalyst Christiane Olivier rightly observes, 'the more violent and perdurable will be the opposition he puts up.'[3] The mother seeks to manipulate him as if he were still a tiny child, and thus leaves him no choice but open rebellion. 'I have a control problem,' says Peter's mother, and that attitude probably accounts for the extreme measures her son took to make himself free. She noticed first the swearing, the greasy dreadlocks and the smell coming off his unwashed body. She told him he could not smoke, and then she found the roof beside the toilet covered in his fag ends. When he was sixteen, he borrowed a large sum of money from a relation and gambled away every penny, which started a pattern of financial delinquency and petty thieving that goes on to this day. Eventually, fed up with his lying and dishonesty, his mother threw him out.

Jason found a more dramatic way of slewing off parental control. He was sixteen and his Catholic family was celebrating Easter. He did not join them, nor did he tell them where he was going. Then, at four in the morning, he woke his parents by stomping around the house. He had come in without any shoes, clearly high on some drug or other and looking like a frightened animal. He said that he was searching for something and would then go out again. His father tried to persuade him to calm down, and bolted the front door against him. Jason rushed downstairs and made for the sitting-room window. 'I am going to live my life the way I want to,' Jason said through his tears. 'I love you both very much but you can't stop me.' Saying that, he went out into the night. His mother later came to realise that it was only in a state of drugged stupor, at an unearthly hour in the morning, that he could tell his parents to back off.

A mother may also try to renew the earlier bonds of physical intimacy. She may walk naked around the house, showing off her luscious curves. She may appear unexpectedly in the bathroom, and take a particular interest in the size of her son's genitals. Occasionally, she may coax him into a full sexual relationship. Or she may, like Karen, take a lover only a few years older than the elder of her two sons, then encourage at least one of her boys to climb into bed with the two of them, so that she can 'have' him by proxy as it were. 'I think it was more fun for the boys in a way,' she says by way of excuse. 'It was better than having a stick-in-the-mud, middle-aged man around.'

When a mother demands intimacy from her adolescent son, the experiences that once made him feel good about himself come to be associated with neediness, causing him to fear that she will never leave him be. He feels sucked under by her emotional pressure, deprived of hope that he can evolve into an independent person with control over his life. Instead of being allowed to break away, he experiences his mother as wanting to swallow him up. Instead of being given his freedom, he feels held. Instead of achieving mastery, he is often destroyed.

The boy wants his mother to reveal that she loves him, wants him, would adore it if he would stay with her for ever, so that he can feel strong enough to leave her. The last thing he needs is for her to do anything that will tie him to her: it is hard enough for him to embrace his freedom without that. That is why he locks his bathroom against her, trying to protect himself and her from the temptation to renew their old intimacy in more adult form. That is why boys feel so threatened by mothers who are flirtatious, and why those who are seduced by their mothers feel such rage towards them.

The son tends to react violently against the mother who tries to hold him. Ted had an intimate physical relationship with his mother until he was in his late teens. He spent a lot of time sitting on her knee, touching her, talking with her. The intimacies of childhood never stopped. He has photographs which show him at the age of sixteen sitting on the beach with his head under his mother's legs. The consequence is that he has spent the rest of his life running away from her. Now, forty years later, when she is in her dotage, he still tells her to mind her own business if she asks him a question, and he tends strategically to lose his way on the journey to her house so as to provide an excuse for the brevity of his visits. 'I am still trying to escape,' he says, 'from this suffocating smother love.'

There are mothers who do not seem too bothered by the imminence of their son's departure. 'It's a natural progression, isn't it,' Lesley says philosophically. 'I cannot understand why people think "This is the end of the world".' But for many others it can be difficult to acknowledge that the bond once broken will never be re-assembled in the same way. What is for him a new opportunity indicates that something is drawing to a close for her. 'My perfect relationship is coming to an end,' remarks Yvonne, a little prematurely, of the life she has with her thirteen-year-old son. 'I have accepted it, but I am mourning inside. I find it really painful to imagine that he will go. That he will just come back occasionally to visit his old mum. It is so sad because this has been the best relationship in my life.'

The mother recognises that, when her son goes, she will

not be needed in the same way again. If she is living without a partner, she may have to face being totally alone for the first time in her life, and reflect mournfully on why she has now been doubly abandoned. If she does not have a satisfying job, she may wonder with regret why she was so willing to give up her career in order to have children. If she is sensible, she will look for some other way to fulfil herself, but any difficulties she faces make it all the harder for her to listen to her son's problems, to enjoy his achievements and to feel happy about the possibilities that lie before him.

Despite feeling sad when a son leaves, the last thing that most mothers really want is for their boys to give up ambition and desire, to hang around the house, treating her just as any little boy treats his mother. Generally, when the son does not show any urge to leave home, the mother takes that as a sign of her failure. So she becomes as irritated with him as his frustration makes him irritable with her. 'What a boring, idiotic life,' Yvonne remarks, 'if he was to stay at home to keep his mother company.' But the mother may be saying, I want you to go, but not just yet. Give me a few more weeks, months, years. Because what she fears is that their relationship will truly be over; that he will sail off to the end of the world, marry some unspeakable woman and never speak to her again.

The aim of the mother-son relationship is to bring about its own redundancy: to enable a young man to live apart from her. If he holds back from taking these final steps, it is because he is afraid. If she seems reluctant to let him go, it is not necessarily because she wants to keep him always beside her, but because this is the final test of her work as a mother. She may well ask herself whether he really has the inner resources to take the knocks that he is likely to endure, to live his life in a way that makes him happy, and to form satisfying relationships with others.

Karen felt anxious about how she would respond when her son took up with his first regular girlfriend. She was relieved to detect no sign of inner conflict when, after leaving her son at a railway station one evening, she looked through the swing doors and saw him kissing a girl on the cheek. But storms of rage and anger did rise when he started his first sexual relationship. Whenever Karen went into her son's bedroom, as it seemed to her, the girl would be stretched out on the bed, with her arms behind her head. 'I don't really care what you think we're up to. He's mine now,' was the message Karen read into this gesture. In reply, she started making nasty comments about the moustache that was springing from the poor girl's upper lip. 'Get that slut out of here,' another mother reported having screamed when her only son took a girl up to his bedroom.

This situation is often made worse by her son's deliberately and provocatively selecting girls who could not be expected to invite mother's approval. 'I think I probably chose girlfriends,' says Eric, 'who were not as middle-class as my parents would have liked them to be.' 'She was an empty-headed, fluffy little thing, rather unintelligent and rather uneducated. We used to laugh at her,' is his mother's unflattering comment on her son's first love. It is difficult for a mother to accept that his choice of girl is determined by his need to break from her, and to make the hurdle less daunting. I will explore this topic further in Chapter Ten, 'Desire for Another'.

Just as the adolescent boy will always be one step ahead of reality, so that the conscientious mother must risk being painted as the demon who holds him back, so the mother of a young adult will tend to be one step behind another reality – that her son really can look after himself without her. There are few things sadder than a mother who cannot accept this, who hangs on to the drops of companionship that her children offer because she has too little else, and who tries still to pull the strings, even when they are married and have kids of their own. She may turn spitefully on her son's chosen wife and spit snide, acerbic remarks into her ear. She may jealously tell all the friends who will listen that her daughter-in-law really is not good enough for her son, the man whom she ensnared.

Most men can dismiss such viciousness as a manifestation of bitterness and incipient senility, but it is much harder to clear out the baggage of fear and anxiety that the same voice stirred when they were much younger. The Chauvinists, who are the subject of the next chapter, show yet again how powerfully a mother's voice can become embedded in the psyches of her sons.

CHAPTER NINE

Chauvinists

Supermarkets are uncharted territory for Felix. He will not go into one or near one, not even into the car park that adjoins one. He sees such places as women's territory, and he does not want anyone to be in any doubt that he is a man.

One Sunday morning, Felix and his wife were driving back from their tennis club. When she asked if they could drop in at the local store to pick up some charcoal for a lunch-time barbecue, Felix replied that he was not going to be the sort of husband who pushed trolleys down the aisles. Lesley reassured him that not even this minuscule step towards New Man status was being asked of him; she would be quite happy for him to stay in the car. He insisted all the same that they drive straight past. She would have to go home, pick up her own car and venture out alone.

On another occasion, just the sight of shopping bags in the car made Felix turn obstreperous and unreasonable. Lesley had gone to collect her husband from the airport. He opened the car boot, found it full of shopping and turned to his wife in a rage. She could not at first imagine what she had done wrong. 'Why did you go to the supermarket on the way here?' he asked.

'We have got to eat,' Lesley quite sensibly replied.

'You could have gone on Monday.'

'Don't be ridiculous,' she said. 'What would we eat over the weekend?'

'Why didn't you go yesterday then?'

'Because I was seeing Melissa for lunch.'

'Even though you knew you had to come and pick me up today.'

'I wasn't late, was I?'

'But you were coming to the airport to pick me up, not to go to the supermarket.'

This conversation contains a clue to Felix's absurd behaviour. He needs his wife's undivided attention, and wants to be continually reassured that she will always be there to take care of him. Travelling home in a car laden with shopping might lead to his being asked if he would kindly help unload the bags. As a next step, he might be cajoled through the automatic doors to pick up a tin of baked beans, then required to negotiate his way through the checkout, after which all would inevitably be lost. Perhaps his wife would take advantage of the revelation that he was not, in fact, completely helpless. She might do his bidding no longer, might even start to follow her own desires, and heaven only knows where that would lead.

'He has always wanted me to himself,' his wife says. She has to be there for him every Friday when he comes off the plane that brings him from his office in Paris. Whenever he is home, he resents attention being given to his children rather than to himself. He loathes it when his wife goes out with a girlfriend and he tried hard, but unsuccessfully, to stop her taking part-time work. He is, or likes people to think that he is, quite incapable of looking after himself. He has never learned to light an oven, fry an egg, sew on a button or lift a duster. Whenever he is apart from his wife, he either visits restaurants or orders food from local take-aways, and then relies upon the daily to clean up after him.

Felix's view of the world is based on the principle

that there should be a firm line of demarcation between men and women. His attitude brings to mind French anthropologist Claude Lévi-Strauss's observation that, in most tribal communities, it is virtually impossible for a man to survive as a bachelor. When staying with the Bororo Indians, Lévi-Strauss recalls, he once enquired about a man of about thirty who was, unlike anybody else in the tribe, unclean, ill-fed and rather sad. What was wrong with him? he asked. The answer came back that he was a bachelor. 'In a society,' Lévi-Strauss wrote, 'where labour is systematically shared between man and woman and where only married status permits the man to benefit from the fruits of woman's work, including delousing, body painting, and hair-plucking as well as vegetable food and cooked food (since the Bororo woman tills the soil and makes the pots), a bachelor is only half a human being.'[1]

Why, though, would any man seek to maintain this sort of situation in a society that increasingly pays lip-service to the idea that there should be equality between the sexes? Does Felix cultivate his dependency, as a feminist might argue, in order to cajole his wife into servicing his needs, so that he can hold on to his patriarchal power? But what is the worth of 'power' that leaves a man so dependent, anxious and ultimately powerless? His wife has only to walk out of the door and he would not know what to do, unless it were to hunt down another woman who would be willing to service him, or to go back and live with his mum.

There is a quality of hysteria about a full-blown Chauvinist that makes one think of a little child sitting on the floor and screaming until his face turns a lurid shade of purple, demanding attention, constantly exaggerating his plight. What the Chauvinist seems most to lack is real confidence in himself. He may be arrogant, pig-headed and domineering, but he does not believe that he can survive without a woman to tend him. This sort of man tends to have grown up in a family where he was not encouraged to develop a sense of his own capabilities in the domestic sphere. He hides behind his masculinity and a definition of gender which promises a guarantee of continued care, in order to guard against his fear of being reduced to a condition of complete helplessness. Any attempt to form a bridge between men and women, to say that the sexes are more similar than they are different, shakes the Chauvinist to the root of his being. Such men tend to emerge from two different sorts of households. Where a mother does everything for her son, the result is the Helpless Chauvinist: where she does almost nothing, she produces the Hungry Chauvinist.

The Helpless Chauvinist had a mother who wrapped him in a cradle of cherishing so as to protect him from the demands of the world. She made herself a slave to the physical and emotional needs of her menfolk. By doing everything for him, never demanding of him that he give her any assistance, she provided her son with no incentive to get off his butt. Her anxious concern conveyed to him that he could not take care of himself, that his safety was completely dependent upon her, that he was impotent without her.

The Hungry Chauvinist, in contrast, strives not to retain what he was used to, but to secure what he has never yet enjoyed. Neglected and abandoned as a child, he always longed for the reassurance that a mother's loving care might have provided. But just securing a woman's declaration of love cannot sufficiently reassure him of his safety; for he is unable to shake off the fear that he is going to lose it. Only if he is almost continuously tended can he feel confident that this woman really does 'love' him.

The mother of the Helpless Chauvinist takes such intense care of him because previous experiences have made her worried about losing male love. Her father may have died when she was very young. She may have almost lost her boy in childbirth, or through a life-threatening illness. She may need a male who will soak up her love, attention and energy, simply because she has never found any other purpose or meaning to her life. She may feel guilty about the treatment he receives from his stern, authoritarian father, and over-compensate by being totally accepting of his demands and his foibles. As a result, she cannot let him out of her sight, nor allow him to do anything that might diminish his need of her.

For Tina, it may have been because her father died in a swimming accident when she was barely three, that she now bestows such intense care upon her husband and her son, hoping to ensure that they do not vanish too. It is also possible that she simply has more energy than she knows what to do with. When I went to visit, she had slept for only a few hours after completing a night-shift at work and then prepared the family tea, but she came to the door exuding warmth and vigour. Her husband, who was sitting on the sofa in his dressing gown, barely managed to nod towards me. Throughout the two and a half hours that I spent with her, a satellite news channel droned on in the next-door room, so that I wondered what it was about the day's events that so held her husband's interest. On the way out, we looked in to see that both Tina's husband and her son Nicholas were lain out on two sofas, sleeping soundly while the television announcer's voice blared out at them.

The Helpless Chauvinist falls into this sort of lethargy because he knows that inactivity is the best way to ensure that everything is done for him. Tina was still putting nappies on Nicholas when he was four: he told her that he preferred not having to get out of bed at night for a leak. When he was nine, he would ask her to bring him a glass of squash, and she would trot obediently into the kitchen, only asking herself when the drink was in his hands why she had jumped out of her seat for a boy who was now tall enough to reach the taps for himself. Now that he is twenty and working in a warehouse (his job aspirations are not pitched very high, since he never passed a single exam in his life), Tina allows Nicholas to live at home without paying rent, provides cash to supplement his meagre wages and drives him to parties. When I ask her how she will encourage him to start looking after himself (and to take more notice of *her* needs) she says to me, 'I cannot stop loving him.'

The Helpless Chauvinist becomes a past master at making excuses for this sort of sloth. Thomas was his mother's youngest son, and, with servants available to handle most domestic tasks, she had little else to do with her time other than taking him with her on tours of the smarter department stores. 'I think my mother was,' he says, 'very indulgent, and surrounded me with love.' Thomas lives now in a flat that stinks and looks as if it might be occupied by a nonagenarian who has been bedridden for the past twenty years. He endlessly says that he is going to clear up the place, but seems quite unable to do anything about it. 'All I have to do at the moment,' he said to me when first I interviewed him, 'is to make my bed, clear away some papers, do some washing-up and sort out the clothes in my bedroom.' This statement significantly under-estimated the amount of work that was required to make the place truly habitable, but when I went to see him again a year later, the smell was worse. He told me then that he could not do anything until the decorators had been, and that this could not happen until a leak had been repaired in the roof. Why did he not just put on a coat of paint one weekend? I asked. Not possible, he replied. 'Firstly, I don't have any paint. Secondly, I don't know how to paint. And thirdly, I don't feel very strong at the moment.'

Needing to keep the spotlight of attention and pity upon himself, so as to ensure that he is taken care of, this sort of Chauvinist is often a hypochondriac. Nicholas first complained of knee pain when he was six and shortly afterwards started to develop headaches. Since then, his mother says, he has laid claim to almost every plausible psychosomatic symptom. On the day of my visit, he had called in the morning to ask if his mother could fix him up with a doctor's appointment. Returning from the surgery, he stomped into the room and reported that, although he had been told to go for tests, he was going to hang on to his blood. I was left with the impression that Nicholas was more nervous about being exposed as a malingerer than concerned about the possibility that the tests would show up something serious.

Thomas, who regularly visits two doctors so that he can compare the verdicts that they give upon his successive complaints, thought it worthwhile to ask me whether I could give him any advice on how to heal his athlete's foot. For most of his maladies – his headaches and his retching coughs – it is all too obvious what the cure might be. Thomas justifies his drinking and smoking as confirming his 'masculinity', even though the real effect is to make him pathetically sick. At first this contradiction perplexed me, until I came to realise how, by keeping him ill, self-neglect helps to ensure that at least one woman, his mother, keeps an eye on him – thus sort of confirming that he is a male. Even now that he is in his late thirties, she will ring his lodger and his doctor to find out how he is doing. Thomas feels angry with her for interfering, complains that she is 'tempestuous, over-aggressive, self-pitying and a bit melodramatic' and asks her to leave him alone, even as he sends out continuous signals that he is having problems. In what he describes as an effort to divert her anxiety, Thomas gives her practical things to do, ordering her to deliver soap, shaving cream, razor blades, shampoo and food to his flat. He would probably ask her to clean the place too, were it not for the fact that she has never scrubbed a floor or wielded a vacuum cleaner in her life.

No relationship looks more like a conspiracy of neediness than that between a Helpless Chauvinist and his mother. But because he recognises how, by doing everything for him, his mother deprived him of any chance to develop his own powers, he tends to angrily blame her for his condition.

'She should have given me more freedom of movement at an early age,' Thomas complains.

Joseph's mother felt during his childhood that she should try to compensate for the many cruelties inflicted upon him by her tyrannical husband. 'I learned to be non-demanding of my children,' she says, 'partly in reaction to this authoritarianism, partly because I wanted a quiet life so that I could get on with other things.' Even though he is now thirty, Joseph lives on at home, reproaching his mother for not having given him the autonomy that he sees as every son's birthright.

Having never made much attempt to live an independent life, Joseph justifies his resentment of his mother by saying that he had been brought up to believe he would one day receive an income from the estate of his wealthy grandfather. For a long time, the money was not forthcoming and, when it did arrive, the amount was, he felt, quite insufficient. Joseph's mother gave him an allowance that might have enabled him to set up on his own, but he decided he would rather stay put. 'I think she was disappointed,' he says, 'that I did not move out, but it is nice to be looked after. I don't pay any rent, there's food in the fridge and I can go to help myself.'

The Helpless Chauvinist is happy to take whatever he considers to be his due, but unwilling to give anything much in return. Joseph lets his mother cook a meal for him on one or two nights a week, but resents even the relatively few duties that fall to him. He has to speak with her, for one thing, even sometimes when he is in the middle of some interesting thought. He must answer the telephone if her friends ring when she is out. And sometimes she calls when she is visiting friends and asks him to carry out some chore that she has forgotten. All of this makes him furious. 'I have been much angrier with her relatively recently,' he says, 'than I can remember being as a child.'

When I asked Thomas whether he ever cooks a meal for

his long-suffering mother, he used the chaotic state of his flat as an excuse for never having done so. He eats meals at his mother's, of course, and lets her buy things for him, but complains when she then asks him questions about his health and his finances. 'Probably,' he says, 'I have been over-indulgent about taking things from her. But I do buy her perfume on her birthday.' Thomas sees his mother's love as a form of non-love. The anxiety and the concern which she feels for him is something that he finds oppressive, and yet he seems powerless to do anything that would make her feel more relaxed about him.

The Helpless Chauvinist's dependency and general sense of powerlessness leave him with an attitude of deep scorn for women. Thomas admits to being a misogynist and says that the word 'women' makes him thinks of peasants in Spanish villages who do all the dirty work while their men drink under a tree. He hates it when women get superior or ratty, because they make him feel 'humiliated'. And when he goes to bed with a woman, even a prostitute, he has a compulsive need to talk about it, even to the most inappropriate people in the most inappropriate situations. Joseph leaves his sex life to my imagination, but I know that he likes to take his holidays in places where the sexual climate is 'liberal' or the girls are pleasingly Oriental. Feeling that women are out to smother and repress him, the Helpless Chauvinist seeks sexual partners whom he can keep well under heel.

The Hungry Chauvinist has to develop an attitude of slightly more sophistication towards women; for it is desperately important to his psychological survival that he find someone who will provide a much more satisfactory relationship than the one he had with his mother. He is more concerned about the danger of losing such a woman than he is anxious about the possibility of his being crushed by her. But he too feels deep down that women are out to destroy him.

Willie had a dreadful relationship with his mother. A

beautiful woman with enormous violet eyes, she had spent the First World War as a motorcycle messenger in France, having racy affairs with men who died in the trenches soon afterwards. Returning to England, she sought out one of the few lovers who had survived, only to find that he was already married and had three children. It was while she was recovering from the nervous breakdown which ensued that she married a portrait painter who had said that he would throw himself off Brighton Pier if she did not become his wife.

The boy who emerged from this ill-starred couple never received much by way of maternal love. His mother told him, in fact, that she wanted nothing to do with him, and shamelessly admitted that, when trying to abort him, she had drunk quite enough gin (the same quantity had worked just fine on a previous occasion), but obviously did not sufficiently heat the water. Apparently preferring a horrid Yorkshire terrier that she clasped to her bosom over Willie, she farmed him out to aunts. He spent his early life trying to win affection and understanding from his mother, but never had any success.

Terry, a furniture remover now in his late thirties, had no contact at all with his mother for several years. She had announced one day that she was no longer willing to endure the 'miserable old sod' who was her third husband, and went off to set up house with another man. From then on she ignored her children, not even taking any action when their father abandoned the two boys into the charge of their elder sisters. For two years, Terry knew nothing about his mother's whereabouts apart from the occasional piece of gossip that he picked up from listening at doors. Even now, he cannot give me a clear answer to my question about how his mother could have abandoned her children. He recalls, though, that the question preyed on his mind so much that he stopped going to school.

For much of their young lives, Willie and Terry longed

for something they were quite powerless to achieve, their mother's love. Having never had a satisfactory relationship with a woman in childhood, it has been very difficult for them to tolerate equality in their later relationships. They are too anxious, too insecure, too frightened; they need to be always in control, because the consequences of allowing someone else to challenge their authority would be to fling them back to the anxieties of childhood.

In order to distinguish himself from the aristocratic social set to which his mother belonged, Willie joined the Communist Party and declared his commitment to feminist ideals. But in practice he ran up against strong internal blocks to implementing sexual equality. Part of the problem derived from his being so ignorant about how domestic tasks were handled, but he seemed also to have an inbuilt resistance to chores. The egalitarian principles that he had discussed with his wife wilted only months into their marriage, as the panic induced by university exams rendered him quite incapable of tackling even a modest share of cooking and cleaning, and the arrangement was never to be reinstated. When his children were teenagers and duties in the house had been allocated by rota, Willie could never remember which week it was, and which duty he was supposed to undertake. And when he was teased about his inadequacies on the domestic front, he would hit his wife.

The same sort of rage at women seems to have motivated Terry's oppression of the childhood sweetheart whom he married when they were both in their teens, but who left him after 22 years together. 'When I think back,' he says, 'I realise that I put this poor woman through hell.' The relationship that Terry describes was marked by a strict division of labour. He expected his wife to keep house while he performed the role of provider. He gave her money to buy food and pay the bills, then demanded that she keep the place clean and tidy. He remembers evenings when he would laze about on the sofa while his wife did the ironing, and times when she was ill in bed and it did not occur to him that it might be nice to offer her a cup of tea. 'I wasn't very helpful,' he says. 'I really didn't take much notice of her. I could have been a lot more caring.'

It was one rule for him, and another for his wife. He insisted upon the freedom to have affairs and to hang out with his mates in the pub. But he required his wife to stay at home even when she had asked him for permission to go out with her sister or on a trip to the coast. 'I trusted her,' he claims, 'but I didn't want her to go. I was very possessive. I wanted to know that when I came home from work she was there.' He justifies himself by saying that he did not want to risk losing his wife, as he had lost his mother, which would have meant putting his kids through what he had to endure. Clearly he had no real faith in her at all.

As he talks, I feel distressed about how little happiness either Terry or his wife can have found in their marriage. They did very little together. He would not go to discos, even though he knew that his wife enjoyed a dance. He would not go for a walk in the park, because his hay fever would cause him to sneeze. And if he suggested going out for an Indian meal, his wife would say that they could not afford it. The sex cannot have been more than mediocre, judging from Terry's account of how he tried unsuccessfully to introduce back home the sexual manoeuvres that he had learned from his mistress. And this married couple were clearly of little use to each other at times of emotional distress. When she felt upset about her grandmother's death, Terry told her not to cry, then sat by helplessly, wondering whether he should cuddle her or not. 'I didn't know the words, what to say to her,' he recalls. Nor was she able to console him when his mother passed away. 'She had the look,' he says, 'of she didn't know what to do.'

And when they discovered that her father had been abusing their nine-year-old daughter, the two of them had no way of talking the thing through. He feared that putting his emotions into words would make him so mad that he would not be able to hold himself back from murder. She felt that he blamed her for what had happened, which he did in a way. A few days after her father's arrest, she took the kids and went off to live with another man. For Terry, the experience stirred up all the anger that he once felt about his mother's leaving but had never been able to acknowledge. He tries not to see his ex-wife now, because he feels that he could not trust himself if he did. 'If I see her,' he says, 'then it all starts coming back. I could really go mad about what she has done.' I ask him to say what he would do to her. 'I wouldn't smash her up,' he says, but his tone does not sound very reassuring. 'I would just get angry and shout. It wouldn't do anybody any good.'

By hitching himself to another woman, the Hungry Chauvinist tries to make up for the deficiencies in his experience of mother, but the impoverishment of his previous experience renders him unable to form an equal, mutually satisfying relationship with his partner. In the next chapter, I will look at how this fits into the general pattern of male desire.

CHAPTER TEN

Man's Desire

What is going on when a man desires a woman or a woman desires a man? Some consider that the answer can be found in genes and hormones; heterosexuality is 'natural' because it is 'procreative'; homosexuality is then explained as the result of a different functioning in the glands, the genes or the brain. This sort of argument, though, is inadequate to explain how biological processes would determine the sex of the object one desires. No one ever suggests that hormones or anything else could decide whether a man prefers big bottoms or tight, narrow ones. How then would they influence whether he prefers to go to bed with a bristly, flat-chested creature who possesses a penis, or someone who has breasts and no facial hair?

Robert Stoller, the author of several important studies of gender identity and sexual perversion, describes heterosexuality as an acquisition. 'We cannot brush the issue aside,' he says, 'by saying that heterosexuality is pre-ordained, necessary for survival of the species and therefore biologically guaranteed. We have no right to accept this unproved, though sensible, biological postulate as being true in humans as in bees or rats.'[1] But if heterosexuality is something that we have to learn, how then do we learn it? I asked a psychotherapist who has been thinking seriously about gender issues for a lot longer than I have if she could give me any tips. 'Who the hell knows what heterosexual desire is about?' she replied. 'I don't get it. How do we understand it? How does it happen? It doesn't really make sense to me.' This declaration of ignorance may not have taken me very far, but it helped to explain why some people cling so hard to arguments from 'nature'.

One 'common-sense' answer to the question might be that it is the experience of being at mother's bosom which shapes the pattern of male erotic desire. Is it not reasonable to suggest that when a man sucks at a woman's breasts, it is because he longs to experience again the joy he felt when taking milk from mother? That when with shivering knees he sidles up to a woman in a bar, it is to recapture again the frisson of being in thrall to a parent who was free to decide whether she would give him pleasure or withhold it. That when he plunges his penis into a woman, he is seeking for a return to the symbiotic union which he enjoyed in his mother's womb and for a short time afterwards. And that when he persuades a woman to marry him, it is with the hope that she will care for him and look after him as his mother once did.

Clearly, it is in the arms of mother (but sometimes father as well) that the boy learns about the pleasure of being in contact with another's body; therefore it is reasonable to argue that desire is at some level an urge to repeat the good experience of mother. The Cuban-American writer Oscar Hijuelos conveys the emotional logic behind this argument in his novel *The Mambo Kings Play Songs of Love*, which traces the loves of two brothers back to the feelings they had about their mother. Nestor is the younger of the two, and his longing for the woman he left behind in Cuba inspires a song 'about love so far away it hurts'. At one point in the book, he calls out, 'Mama, I wanted Maria the way I wanted you when I was a baby feeling helpless in that bed, with welts covering my chest, and lungs stuffed with thick cotton. I couldn't breathe, Mama, remember how I used to call you?'[2]

Several writers suggest too that it is because men secure such 'nearly perfect care'[3] in the arms of their mothers, that they are often so restless in their relationships. They cannot see a woman as she is, but only as a stand-in for their mother. They expect to find someone who will give without expecting anything in return, loving them without criticism or rancour, and all the problems in their relationships start from the fact that they are landed instead with a woman who has as many needs as they do, who can be querulous, demanding and needy, who seeks from her lover and her husband not a baby to mother, but a father to raise her up.

Explaining male heterosexual desire as an attempt to repeat the experience of mother immediately gives rise to a question: why then are not all women lesbians? Do not they too suck at their mother's breasts? Do they not have the same experience of a mother's loving care and overweening power? Why then do they not all long for a relationship with an adult woman in which they can recapture their infantile experience of being loved and mastered by mother. Some do argue that this is exactly what all women really want; to relive their experience of being 'mothered'. Only social convention and patriarchal power force them into heterosexual relationships, even though these are inherently unsatisfactory because men are so bad at 'mothering'. If this argument were to be widely accepted, men would either have to change themselves double quick or to accept that opportunities for satisfying their desires were in terminal decline. However, such an outcome seems unlikely: it cannot explain the many dimensions of women's desire for men.

Another problem with the argument that a man's desire for a woman expresses his longing to re-experience mother is that one might expect this to result in some sort of connection between the satisfactoriness of the initial experience and the strength of the desire. The better it was with mother, the more you would long to repeat the experience. If a boy's mother was cold and distant, he would be less committed to heterosexuality than the man who spent his childhood in a loving swoon. But it is because he feels a deficient connection to mother that the Lovelorn Son precociously starts wanting to fling himself into the arms of another woman. The less rewarding his experience of mother, this suggests, the stronger is the man's yearning for someone else to take her place. 'I remember when I was five,' says Gus, who used to find his mother's criticisms and rages hard to endure, 'just holding a pillow tight and thinking it would be nice to have someone there. I suppose that I wanted a wife.' And for the son who never felt that he was loved by mother, the experience of eventually making contact with a woman can be explosively wonderful because so unprecedented. 'That first proper kiss,' wrote writer and broadcaster Ludovic Kennedy in his memoirs, 'that intimate physical contact was for me like a sort of cloudburst, for not only had I found for the first time a woman to love but – far more important and also for the first time – a woman who was actively loving me.'[4]

The heterosexual male seems to be searching less for what mother actually provided, the 'almost perfect' experience described so often, than for what she might have offered. The man wants a better experience of mother than he had in reality, as well as a chance to simultaneously re-experience all the good elements from the past. This would seem to be what is described in the Freudian idea that there is something incomplete about the boy's relationship with his mother, because what he wants is to take his father's place in his mother's bed. Learning that he cannot do this, he sets out to find the next best thing, another woman whom he can treat as he would have liked to have treated his mother.

The argument that the adult is looking for a more satisfactory experience than he had before is useful for understanding female desire as well. Women are less interested in what they had from mother than in what they might have received from their fathers. Most (but not all) girls experience their father as providing much less physical and emotional warmth than their mothers, but his occasional presence may be experienced as thrilling and deeply satisfying. It has often been observed that fathers provide their children with more stimulating play than mothers. They tend to fling them in the air, push them up trees and take them down the scarier runs at theme parks. The downside of such exposure to father is that, because so intermittent, it feeds a hunger that can never be satisfied. The daughter feels that she does not get enough of dad. She comes to believe that if only she could have what mother has, then her longing would be fulfilled. Why not, then, try for a more continuous exposure to male excitement through a heterosexual experience?

Observation of the general pattern in relationships seems to confirm how the traditional style of parenting imprints itself on the expectations that men and women have of each other. The man draws away from the woman who wants to come closer. Men, who generally have so much of mother, tend to experience her presence as sometimes smothering, stifling and demanding. In their later relationships, the pull towards intimacy and sexual union is powerfully countered by the fear of being submerged or swallowed up. They cannot get close because they do not think they will survive the experience. Women, on the other hand, seem often to be reaching out to bring men in, to stop them being so absent, distant and separate. They want from their current man what they did not have before, what it sometimes seems that no man can give them.

Yet this cannot be a satisfactory explanation of hetero-sexuality either. Boys also have unsatisfactory relationships with their fathers. Why should they fix on the maternal side of the parenting equation as the one for which they need to compensate? Why is it not just as important for men to try for a more satisfactory form of fathering through relationships with men? Why do not both sexes seek to make up for the unsatisfactoriness of their two parents by being openly bisexual?

In early adolescence this *is* how many boys do seem to experience their sexuality, as something focused on both sexes. Just as gender identity is usually amorphous in the first years of life, so too it seems that sexual orientation takes time to settle down. Boys want boys, they want girls, they are hungry for any sort of sexual contact. What the adolescent knows is a confusion of desires, a series of messages about longing and lusting that he cannot properly interpret. And then, for most but not for all, their sexuality tends to become more defined, channelled towards one sort of object rather than the other.

It could be argued – and it has been – that this is simply the result of social inhibition and repression, that it is only because heterosexuality is the norm within the families in which most people mature, and is ordained as 'natural' because it fosters the reproduction of the species, that so many people go along with it. While this may explain those who enter marriage while recognising, dimly or otherwise, that their true desires are for the other gender, it hardly accounts for the strength of the commitment that most people feel to their sexual orientation. Nor does it explain why boys who grow up within a lesbian couple often turn out 'straight'.

There are homosexual boys who recall explicitly sexual desires being felt towards members of their own sex when they were four or five, in a way that suggests their orientation might have been defined at the same time as they came to recognise themselves as being of one sex rather than the other. This may be true of others too, even though they do not know it. The boy who experiments with different partners could be seen as trying to find out what he is, rather than deciding what he wants to be. Adolescence is like receiving the results of an exam that you completed some time earlier and had almost put out of your mind, but which you recognise will decisively shape your future.

I argued in Chapter Four that boys feel unhappy about having to accept their single gender. Seeing the attraction of both positions, they regret being pushed into adopting one identity rather than the other by the unchangeable fact of their genital equipment. Childhood is then taken up with attempts to convince themselves that the position so prescribed for them is by far the best, as they attempt to find out what is meant by the gender role that has been laid down. Since that is his destiny, he needs to know what it means to be male, but he remains quite interested in what it is like to be female. This does not seem like much of a problem in his early years. There are, after all, all sorts of ways in which, by identifying with the more impressive aspects of mother, he can experience femininity.

Puberty, though, shatters any sense that there is a fluid line between the gender positions. The transformations that hormones now induce upon his own body and those of his female contemporaries, girls who were once so much more like him, forcefully increase his awareness of the differences between the sexes. Together with his own genital development, the observation of how his female contemporaries have changed stimulates his erotic interest. Fully recognising for the first time that he will never be inside a female skin, there is only one way left for him to experience the sort of physical femininity with which he is now confronted, and that is through sex. I remember when I was twelve arguing with a school-mate that it was stupid to waste time kissing girls who had not yet developed breasts. It was only when they had filled out on top that they had anything special to offer. A few months later, I became obsessed with a girl some few years older than myself whose mammary fullness was her most striking characteristic, and in whose presence I was absolutely speechless.

The boy sets out, then, on a quest for access to women's bodies and an opportunity to negotiate the line between his maleness and her femaleness. With each inadvertent erection and every passing sexual thought, he is reminded of the difference between them, the chasm that he has to cross. Unsurprisingly, he feels daunted by the challenge. 'No woman has to prove herself a woman in the grim way a man has to prove himself a man,' says Camille Paglia, that high-priestess of bombast and celebrant of raw masculinity. 'He must perform or the show does not go on. Social convention is irrelevant. A flop is a flop.'[5] What Freud dubbed castration anxiety might just as easily have been called performance anxiety.

It is sometimes suggested that, given the extent of his intimacy with mother, a man should find it easy to move into a physical relationship with a woman. But cuddling mum and penetrating another woman are not comparable activities. Closeness to mother does not preclude his being terrified of crossing into the land of fulfilled desire. Indeed, the fact that he has been so involved with mother, while recognising that intercourse with her was taboo, may make this step even more daunting. Joe, who is thirteen, feels so shy when he fancies a girl that he can only deal with the situation by getting to know one of her friends. 'As soon as I stop desiring someone,' he says, 'then I am no longer shy with them.' One reason for this, he says, is that he feels guilty about betraying his mother, to whom he is close, with someone else.

This sense that having sex is a form of treachery may be another reason why so many men feel the need to take up initially with someone who is strikingly different from their mothers. They do not want to be reminded of her while embarking on their first sexual experiments. Michael, for example, challenged his mother's prissy and conventional outlook on life by becoming engaged to a vivacious Spaniard whose religion, nationality and age (somewhat older than his own) all appalled his mother. But he quickly realised that this was not an ideal basis for a life-long partnership, and broke off the engagement. While the young man's desire to make up for mother's shortcomings and accidental cruelties takes him away from her, his wish to refind the good experience of mother draws him towards a woman who is like her.

It is because the feelings evoked by intimacy can be so

fearful that many boys cultivate a mechanistic attitude to sex. Intercourse is seen as no more than a testing and re-testing of the genital equipment. When Sean was thirteen and went into a meadow with a class-mate, the fact that he did not even like her had no impact upon her eligibility to become his first lover. 'She was ugly,' he recalls, 'but she had big tits and she did it, which not many did at that age. It was just something you had to do, like having your first cigarette or getting drunk.' For Tony, the attraction of the first girl he went to bed with was that she was 'common', which meant that she was 'easy-going'. For a few years after that, he took his kicks from seeing how many girls he could score within a week: three was his goal. All that mattered to him was demonstrating that he could do it and thus prove he was a 'man'.

Although some men continue all their lives to regard women as nothing more than bags of flesh whom they can take to bed (or into a field), screw and discard, so that the ideal relationship is one with a prostitute who will make no other demand than that her fee be paid, most eventually formulate a desire to satisfy deeper emotional needs and longings. This moving-on mirrors the usual pattern of development in the mother-son relationship. Sexual coupling takes the boy back to the ecstatic glow of the first intimacy with mother, while the next stage in a relationship re-opens the more complex negotiation over merger and independence through which he forged his character and personality.

Sex offers a man the opportunity to break down the boundaries, throw off the burden of self and relapse into a state of de-individuation. He can make contact again with emotions that have been blocked off for a long time, because he did not feel it was safe to experience them in the presence of his mother. He has a chance to find again the perfect mother he never had, someone who will understand him completely, love him absolutely, and make him feel at ease with himself. Reality, of course, never sustains for very long the weight of such a fantasy.

Yet if sex is an opportunity to bridge the gap between men and women, that bridge is one across which an enemy can all too easily pass. What is for a time pure pleasure brings back eventually the feelings with which it was also associated, of being helpless, dependent and in thrall. Falling in love forces men to confront again the needs they had of mother, and her failure to satisfy them. At the same time as a man rediscovers the 'good' mother, he also brings up the 'bad' whom were experiences as engulfing, manipulative and dangerous. The more powerful his experiences of this 'bad' mother were in the past, the more easily will she be evoked by other women, and the more likely it is that he will see danger in even well-meant words and gestures from the person with whom he shares a bed. In their relationships with women, men continue a contradictory search for merger with another from whom they can remain separate.

A man can react to these feelings in two ways. He may decide that the 'bad' mother is always going to be acting out her baleful and dangerous desires, so that the only way to maintain his sense of self is by keeping a distance from women. For fear of what might happen, he will feel impelled to cut himself off from full intimacy. Alternatively, he can seek to master his terrors and anxieties by learning to trust the women with whom he is linked. Most men adopt a combination of these strategies. Their relationships become battles over boundaries, in which they try to see how close they can come to the 'good' mother who cherished them without stirring up the 'bad' mother who threatened to destroy them.

What, then, does a man look for in his partner? If it were simply a person who did not provoke his fears, all men would seek out someone who was compliant, weak and altogether pathetic – a woman whom they could easily dominate. Male desire, though, is usually more complex than that. A man wants to experience the spark of battle together with the comfort of safety. He seeks a woman who will make him feel afraid, and then enable him to prevail, who will challenge him and then let herself be conquered, provoke him and then surrender.

Most men want a relationship that is set upon a tightrope. They thrive when the essential conflict is sustained, when they feel neither totally safe nor overly threatened. A man wants to be able to surrender himself to ecstatic sexual passion without feeling that he is going to be devoured in a monster's maw, yet knowing that there is some danger. He wants to be in control and yet simultaneously out of control. He wants to prove that he can survive the danger, but he does not want to be so endangered that he might not survive. He wants a powerful woman whom he can dominate, not just a woman who does what she is told, never ventures an opinion of her own, eagerly seeks to serve her man at all times. If he does not feel a slight possibility that he could lose everything, that he must be continuously vigilant, then he will see no reason to stay. That said, of course, the effort and the anxiety involved will often make him insecure, angry and distressed. 'Am I strong enough to withstand the risks of intimacy with this person?' he will ask himself. 'Can I go on having my needs satisfied by her?' And if the answer seems to be 'No', then he may lash out in fury.

As I will explore further in the next chapter, many men are incapable of finding a balance that works for them. Because these Idolaters experience their mothers as so overwhelmingly strong, they oscillate unhappily between two extremes, between a woman who is much less powerful than they, makes them feel great for a while, and then leaves them feeling bored because she never challenges them, and the dominatrix who wants them as her slave. For a while they happily surrender to a woman's power, but eventually they have to throw off the chains she has put around them. Homosexuality can be seen as a way of resolving this dilemma, of escaping the threat that mother poses by coupling with a man.

One plausible way of explaining why some men feel drawn

towards experiencing sexual and emotional intimacy with a person of the same sex as themselves is that, because of their childhood background, such men experience the male as more 'other' than the female and therefore more intriguing, the sex they want to know about even though it is their own. And their experience of mother renders them more sensitive to the risk of being swallowed up by a woman if they were to become intimate with her. They feel as a result safer with a man, more confident that they can maintain their sense of separateness.

Studies have repeatedly shown that gay men tend to have had an extremely close bond to their mothers, but to feel distant from their fathers. Many heterosexual men experience something similar, but when June talks about the connection she feels to her gay son Irwin, it is of something fundamentally different than was stirred by her second (straight) boy. Irwin seemed to enjoy the music that she played, to like the things that she liked and to want closeness with her. The relationship has been 'pally' ever since he was in his early teens, and even now, when he is making his living as an actor, the two of them enjoy meeting for a gossip. 'He is like me in a way,' she feels. 'She is,' he says, 'the only person I can let myself sob in front of.' His sense of being, by contrast, fundamentally different from his father may have helped him to realise that it is possible (and desirable) to enjoy difference within a homosexual relationship. Freed from any sexual undertones, he does not feel tested, challenged, undermined, exposed or endangered when in his mother's company, and he can embrace his similarity to her, without any of the sense of danger that a straight man experiences.

It is impossible to say whether it was Irwin's disposition which created the possibility of such a bond developing, or his mother's neediness that caused her to embrace him as an object of special affection. Those who believe in the existence of a gay gene might argue for the first alternative, that a boy is born with a disposition that shapes the feelings he has towards his mother and his own sex, but it would be possible to argue that it was the mother's feelings towards her son which determined his mature sexual orientation. The antithesis is probably over-simplistic, and in reality there is probably an interaction between the child's chemical makeup and the influence of those to whom he feels close which together combine to shape the direction of his sexual desire.

It is wrong anyway to take too rigid a perspective on the dividing line between straight and gay. The most pressing human need is for a relationship to another. Childhood experiences help to determine whether that intimacy is experienced as more exciting, and yet safe, when it is with a woman or a man. It might be possible to re-negotiate that position as one passed through life, but few do because the desire to declare oneself one thing rather than the other encourages most to cling until death to the label they first put upon themselves.

CHAPTER ELEVEN

Idolaters

Norman is a gentle bear of a man in his early sixties, with the sort of ruddy complexion that reveals a love of food and wine. His raunchy sense of humour provides many opportunities for him to show off a glorious, bellowing laugh, and his vitality is such that I am a little surprised when he tells me that there is one of life's pleasures which he has not enjoyed, because he is a virgin. He credits his condition to a lifelong fear that, if he were to go too close to a woman, he would end up as pallid and diminished a man as his father was.

It was when he was five that he first remembers sensing his dad was not all he might have been. They had arrived at Cape Town on a ship that was taking the family back to their home in Dar-Es-Salaam. Norman set out with his father to reach the summit of Table Mountain. The two of them had just completed the first stage of the ascent when Norman's father looked up at the wires supporting the cable car and pronounced that they would not be going any further. It is an incident that, even now, Norman recalls with disgust. 'I just remember,' he says, 'being bitterly disappointed, and thinking he was a wimp.'

Shortly afterwards, Norman was sent back to England,

where he was to spend three years in boarding school, fantasising what domestic life would be like when his parents returned from Africa for good. He imagined his father running a large household, as he had done in the colonies, and driving around in a big car. The reality, as it turned out, was to be very different. Not only was Norman's father unable to secure gainful employment and consequently without access to even a single servant or any sort of automobile, but the effect upon his health of those years spent in the tropics began to show. Norman remembers him lying in bed with malarial fever, and retching as a result of the migraines from which he also suffered.

Norman's father began to behave very oddly, becoming obsessed with cleanliness and with filing, which he called 'putting things in datal order', and he would ramble endlessly on about his 'guilt' for everything that had happened to the family. Gradually his stability began to crumble; he had a breakdown and was placed in a mental institution. Norman recalls visiting his father in a ward full of gibbering wrecks, reached down a dark brown corridor that seemed to stretch for miles and reeked of carbolic and piss. There he lay, weak and wan, down to half his weight, with his eyes sunk into his head, agitated, suicidal, paranoid and apparently dying of pneumonia.

Against these images of his father as a broken husk, Norman remembers his mother as a woman 'without equal'. She was the sort of kind, generous, warm-hearted person towards whom people gravitated as they would to a blazing log fire. He remembers her reading Grimm and Hans Andersen to him, playing the piano beautifully and filling the house with joy, in striking contrast to his father's obsessive fastidiousness. She could, though, be somewhat shrewish, and once described to him an occasion on which she had humiliated his father sexually. Although this was hardly enough to suggest that she might have had some responsibility for the disastrous decline in her husband's well-being, Norman found sufficient evidence elsewhere to suggest that women could be extremely dangerous.

On one occasion during his lonely and unhappy years at boarding school, he had been beaten for thinking that he could go to Sunday lunch at the house of a friend's mother without having previously asked permission from the headmaster. Sent weeping to his bed, he took up a copy of *David Copperfield* in the hope that he could drown his sorrows by reading about experiences more horrible than his own. Suddenly, the headmaster's wife appeared at the door, screaming that a boy who was in disgrace had no right to read novels. 'She was a witch,' Norman recalls, 'a most terrifying woman, who had the most frightful rages.'

Two other viragos made a strong impression on Norman, significantly at a time when, now in his mid-twenties, he was actively thinking that he ought to find a wife. One was the mother of a friend who had said he could park his car outside her house, giving him the impression that this was to be a regular arrangement when in fact she considered it only a one-off. A few days later, when Norman was getting into his motor, she came out of the gate and subjected him to an intense verbal drubbing about his selfishness and his arrogance. 'Why the hell,' she screamed, 'should we put up with your car sitting next to our kitchen window?' Norman recalls feeling sick to the bottom of his stomach at the sight of the woman he had formerly considered a friend viciously shouting at him over what was, after all, only a misunderstanding.

The other virago was someone who became, for a short time and with extreme reluctance on her part, his prospective mother-in-law. When this woman learned that her daughter was planning to wed a man who was, at the time, a mere employee in the planning department of the city council, and whose father was a mental patient, she let it be known that, if the marriage were to go ahead, her daughter had no option but to elope. The girl's father responded in a more conciliatory fashion by trying to fix Norman up with a better-paid job. Norman's decision to turn it down inspired from the mother a torrent of recrimination so violent that it put him in mind of no one so much as the headmaster's wife.

But Norman was more significantly affected by the husband's response: this architect whose success Norman admired, whom he had almost adopted as an alternative father-figure, began to blubber and, through his tears, to plead that his prospective son-in-law should take the post which had been offered. Suddenly the dynamic of the marriage was exposed. This man was yet another weakling in thrall to his domineering wife. He needed Norman to do his bidding, because he was powerless to prevail against her. All Norman's childhood fears were evoked anew: marriage, the evidence suggested, could only destroy men. He broke off the engagement a few weeks later without any serious regrets.

It was to be ten years before Norman was to risk a second humiliation at the hands of a woman. In the intervening period, he channelled his energies into work, persuading himself that, given his father's shocking physical and mental deterioration, it might be just as well if he, the progeny of such tainted stock, did not marry and produce a family. But he had begun to feel dissatisfied, to wonder if there might not be more to life than his daily toil at the drawing board and enthusiastic participation in the church choir. When he met a woman who had recently separated from her husband, with whom he quickly came to establish a strong rapport, he started to visit her on two evenings a week. After putting her two children to bed, they would eat dinner and spend an hour or so canoodling on the sofa. A man of strong religious beliefs, Norman was not inclined to go any further towards sexual coupling.

On one occasion, though, Naomi, the woman concerned, persuaded Norman to put aside his trousers and his underpants. He was about to enter her when caution got the better of him. Clearly not amused, Naomi did not hold back her resentment. Putting Norman under steadily greater pressure to show more commitment to the relationship, she made him feel that he was being pushed around. Then, one evening when she had dragged him to the sofa and found that he was still reluctant, she snarled at him, 'You don't even know where it is.' No remark was better calculated to remind Norman of what his mother had once said about her treatment of his father.

Another ten years were to elapse before Norman's third and final humiliation. He fell for a woman whom he had met while staying with a friend in Connecticut. Rooming arrangements made it impossible for them to try sleeping together on that visit: so Norman returned the following Christmas and, at the age of 45, made his first serious attempt to have a full sexual relationship. Whether because of the tranquillisers he was taking at the time, shyness about his sexual inexperience or some other cause, his genital apparatus was unwilling. 'It went completely flop,' Norman recalls, 'and I was mortified beyond belief.'

On New Year's Eve, towards the end of his stay, Norman was to make one final effort to deliver sexual satisfaction. He had taken no drugs for days and everyone else in the house had been sent off to various parties, so that there would be no distractions. After enjoying a meal together, they removed their clothes and embraced. Fireworks were exploding outside and the penile member rose for action. Things looked promising indeed at the point when Norman gazed ahead and saw a gigantic Alsatian standing in front of him: it had come in through a kitchen door that had accidentally been left open, in flight from all the noise. By the time that Norman's would-be lover had coaxed the animal outside, all thought of sex had passed from his head. 'Are you sure you're not homosexual?' the disappointed woman asked.

'Well, I'm not completely sure,' he replied.

'Why don't you go and see if you prefer that?' she said,

effectively terminating for life Norman's ambition to form a sexual relationship.

Norman's problem, though, lay not so much in any doubts he might have about his sexual orientation, it was rather that he had no image of male fortitude to set against his experience of mother. He grew up pining for her love and approval, recognising the power that she had over him. And when he looked for his father to provide him with the evidence that he could break away, survive and obtain the same satisfactions from someone else, he found that there was no one there, or rather someone so debilitated as to make him more afraid for his future than confident about it.

So much is written about male power that it is often overlooked how much more significant in a boy's experience is his mother's suzerainty. The man of the house, assuming that there is one at all, may hold the purse strings, dominate the conversation at dinner time, or come home from the pub on Saturday night to beat his wife into a suppurating pulp, but it will still be the mother's presence and authority to which her son is most exposed. In comparison with her, father is inactive, uninvolved, absent. He is no use to a boy who is trying to work out how he can be strong in the face of such feminine potency. He may learn how to seduce and charm his mother, but he will never quite manage to prevail against her. And the boy whose father is broken and dispirited will not only feel that he lacks an ally, but will find it hard to develop any confidence in his own capacity to do what his father has so patently failed to: take on his mother's overwhelming might.

In order to avoid his father's fate, Norman worked hard to win his mother's approval, doing at school all the things that gave her pleasure. He played the organ, sang in the choir, acted in school plays, became chairman of the debating society and won a university scholarship. He then discovered that, in the light of his own triumphs, his uneducated father's condition looked all the more pitiful. 'It really comes back to that classic adolescent fight between father and son,' he says. 'Who is cock of the dung heap? I am afraid that I won, which was very bad both for him and for me.' It was bad because, by usurping his father in his mother's affections, he increased his own anxieties that the man's depleted state might eventually be his own.

The son in this position takes his mother's side and absorbs her example, not because this seems the most attractive of the two options, but because he has no choice if he is to assure his survival. The relationship that Norman had with his mother was warm enough to create few initial problems. The situation was much harder for Harold, a civil servant now in his early thirties, who experienced his father as 'not strong' and his mother as inattentive, unjust and all-powerful.

Harold's mother enrolled him in the primary school where she taught, because that was the most convenient arrangement for her. She there upset her son on several occasions by barely acknowledging him when they passed in the corridor, and by more generally failing to recognise the problems that resulted from his being a teacher's son. Identified as such, Harold became the class's prime candidate for victimisation. On one occasion, a group of his peers blocked the toilets with loo paper and then fingered him with the responsibility. His mother paid no attention to Harold's pleas of innocence or his claim that he had been unjustly punished, and did nothing to right the wrong that had been done.

The image that an indignant Harold retained of his mother after that was reinforced by a later experience. He was at home with the daily help during half-term when he decided to swap the copper in his piggy bank for silver from his mother's store. He thought that he had calculated the figures correctly, but when his mother came to check them, they did not tally. She told Harold to confess that he had deliberately stolen from her, but he again insisted upon his innocence. She replied that he had committed a serious offence, which would lead to her calling the police if he did not own up straightaway, but even the threat of prison did not cause Harold to change his story. Despatched to his bedroom, he pulled the bedclothes tight around him and waited for the awful spanking that his mother eventually came to inflict upon him.

In all these battles with his mother, Harold felt that his father was no use. He might appeal to him for justice, demand of him that he ensure reason prevail, but he always knew that his calls would go unheeded. His father had put himself in the background and there he was going to stay. Thus does the Idolater learn that, if he is not to be destroyed by mother, he must appease her by worshipping and never challenging her. Otherwise he will risk being swept away by her ensuing wrath.

When he starts trying to form a relationship with another woman, the Idolater often finds himself trapped between two unsatisfactory solutions. He can hitch himself to someone who is challenging, sexually exciting, full of drive, determination and guts, whom he worships as he did his mother, but who can be expected to leave him feeling depleted and overwhelmed. Alternatively, he can find someone timid, undemanding and supportive, someone who makes him feel safe, with whom he will risk feeling a little bored, wishing that he was braver and stronger.

I met Harold through one of his former girlfriends, who long after they had broken up would still call him whenever she needed her plumbing mended or her car taken into the garage or someone to collect her from the airport. How, I wondered, could a man be quite so tame? Harold says that he now wants a relationship in which he has some control, much more than his father ever had, but he also wants someone who will stimulate him in a way that only a woman like his mother could. He never can find the right sort of person. For a time he will enjoy being with someone who is 'weak, defenceless and pathetic', but eventually her passivity will drive him crazy. 'I tend,' he says, 'to be intrigued, interested in and excited by women who have authority and know what it is that they want,' but then the moment arrives when he realises to what degree he has surrendered his own authority. How, he asks himself, can he be in control and yet submit to the control of another?

Whether a woman is weak and needy, or strong and domineering, she has the same power over the Idolater whom she can compel to her will. Whether he is reaching down to help up a forlorn woman, or responding to the whip that is wielded above him, he is always doing the bidding of another. That is what he is used to, the only sort of relationship that he understands.

Unlike Harold, Mike did not even have a father to whom he could vainly appeal for support. Now a psychiatrist in his late thirties, he learned to see his mother as a martyr to the callous irresponsibility of men, particularly to the man who had abandoned her. She was a 'hero' who had sacrificed her life for her children and done a pretty good job of bringing them up. His father, by leaving the family home when Mike was in the womb, had behaved in a way that could only be judged akin to murder.

Mike's mother also made him feel more than a little afraid that she might one day go through the door much as his father had done and never return. His childhood memories reflect this fear of being abandoned. He recalls walking between the chestnut trees in a local park, watching his mother and brother several paces ahead, and panicking because he thought they might be about to leave him behind. And he remembers lying in bed at night, calling out to his mother and wondering what he would do if she were to disappear.

The deficiencies of his father render the Idolater totally dependent upon his mother. He is so much aware of the precariousness of his position if he was in any way to anger her that he dare not do so. He must hold on to the 'good' mother and he is more than a little frightened of stirring up the 'bad' one, she who might destroy him. He cannot risk a relationship that is open and freely negotiated, because he is conscious that this might lead to his elimination. He is not likely to carry much clout in his adult relationships. Mike's mother confirms this when she says of his present girlfriend that she has complete control over him. 'I tell him,' she says, 'that he must stand up to her just once. It does not matter what on, just on something.' When she asked him once why he could not do this, he gave her a chillingly honest reply, 'I am frightened of her, mother.'

Mike told me that his childhood experiences have left him incapable of saying 'No' to a woman. This sense of powerlessness meant that, when he formed his first serious relationship, at the age of twenty-two, it was with someone who lived and worked in Stuttgart on the other side of the English Channel. They met only during the school holidays, when she came to stay. Mike enjoyed knowing that he was loved, but he could only feel safe if his girlfriend was 'there but not there'.

After eight years, his girlfriend Ulrike became restive with this arrangement and began to push for something closer. She came to London for a year as an exchange teacher and then announced that she wanted to have a baby. This was not at all what Mike had in mind. He replied that this was an unwise move at a time when they had not established a permanent home, defensively ignoring the likelihood that it was Ulrike's desire for this to happen that had partly motivated her desire to become pregnant. 'If you don't give me a baby,' she then said, 'I will have one with somebody else.'

Lacking the capacity to simply refuse, Mike did not know how to deal with this ultimatum. He was not ready to start a family, nor to walk away from the relationship. He felt trapped between two impossible courses of action. There was a voice which told him to short-circuit his dilemma, behave like a man and be completely upfront about his desire not to have a child at that point of time. His girlfriend might have respected him if he could have been so clear about things, but he did not have the courage to follow the thought through. Instead, the voice which won said that he would be behaving abominably if he did not give his girlfriend what she wanted. After all, they had been together for eight years.

Instead of acting or speaking decisively, Mike played a messy double game. He did nothing to prevent Ulrike from becoming pregnant, but nor did he declare a full commitment to her. Then, in order to prove to himself that he was sort of in control of his own life, he started an affair with another woman, justifying this to himself as being his 'last fling'. He could not fully acknowledge to himself his doubts about the course that Ulrike had taken. And when she did become pregnant, he remembered the view that his mother had expressed about men who abandoned their children, and signed up for marriage.

The marital arrangements quickly became a farce. Mike carried on in London while Ulrike stayed with her parents and the child in Stuttgart. Their meetings were so strained that they never once had sex as man and wife, so that the marriage which had produced a child remained technically unconsummated. And his anger with Ulrike for having manipulated him came out not directly, but in the feelings that were stirred up in him by his baby girl. While Ulrike was pregnant, Mike longed for her to have a miscarriage. After a daughter had been born, he hoped that she might become sick and die. Sometimes he even thought that he might kill her himself.

In all his battles with Ulrike, Mike seems to have been trying both to do the honourable thing that would win his mother's approval, and to follow his own fears and desires, which would have led him in quite the opposite direction, but it was always the maternal angle that won out. His mother's threat of ostracism if he did not stick it out with his wife and daughter had such a powerful influence upon him that he was completely unable to end the forlorn relationship, so that it was eventually Ulrike who asked for a divorce. The paradox was that, by obeying his mother's commandments, Mike ended up committing the greatest crime that he could commit in her eyes: he abandoned his child.

The most promising strategy for the Idolater is to acquire some of the strength he sees in his mother. Oliver is a drag queen who has always felt very much drawn towards his mother's model of life. He describes his father as 'sweet but infuriatingly passive', which is the sort of description that many Idolaters would give. Dad was a 'nice' man who took Oliver to the swimming baths and to the cinema, but whose gentleness would sometimes give way to vicious fury as he flung pots, pans and other implements around the kitchen. On these occasions, Oliver would stand ready to take his mother into his arms and console her, only to feel disappointed when she ran to speak with the next-door neighbours.

Like every Idolater, Oliver felt towards his mother a combination of fear and awed admiration. On the one hand, he has made the celebration of her inner strength into the centre of his night-club act, in which he projects himself as a Barbra Streisand-type who can take a lot of knocks and come back singing, just as he feels his mother has always done. 'For all her strengths and insecurities,' he says, 'she is a hugely strong woman who has overridden all the things that have come at her. She has accomplished a lot in her life.'

Oliver also, on the other hand, had sufficient experience of his mother as an unstable, vicious witch to feel nervous about intimacy with a woman. He recalls how, when he was six, and competing with a friend to see whose pee could go furthest down an alleyway, his mother came up from behind, grabbed his hair and called him a 'disgusting boy'. She then dragged him home, his trousers still around his ankles, screaming at the top of his voice. Several years later, Oliver invited some friends to a bonfire night party in the garden of their house. When his mother discovered that one of these friends was using an aerosol to create columns of fire, she ran through the garden, screaming 'Who has got a flame-thrower?' Oliver rushed to intercept her and push her back into the house, but she broke free. Oliver went back to his bedroom, barricaded the door and stayed there for the rest of the night. 'I wanted her to be a proper mother,' Oliver recalls, 'nice and normal like everybody else's mother.'

One way of looking at the attitude of many homosexuals to their mothers and to other women is as successful Idolatry. They worship but do not touch. (This says nothing about how they construct their relationships to male lovers.) Aware of his mother's power and his father's uselessness, feeling very close to his mother and distant from his father, the homosexual man sides with her and never tries to shift towards the male position. He feels at one with his mother, however irritating she may sometimes be, and is as much intrigued by the mystery of his father as any daughter. His mother's displays of strength convince the homosexual Idolater that he should placate her in every way; her hysteria warns him off adopting his father's position and exposing himself to all her baleful powers.

Freed from any desire to have intercourse with a woman, the homosexual is then able to enjoy a relationship of relaxed friendliness with mother of a sort that no heterosexual can quite achieve. So normal does this seem to him that he does not realise how strange it appears to (heterosexual) outsiders. Ben, for example, never thought much of his stepfather, and was severely rebuffed when, at sixteen, he tried to make contact with his biological father, but even now he speaks to his mother over the telephone every other day. There is no sense of duty about it; he just likes making contact, even though he describes as 'garbage' what they say to each other. 'How has your day been?' he will ask. 'I saw so-and-so,' she will reply. 'He sends his love.' She will then recount the ups and downs of her somewhat desiccated marriage. He will tell her what he is doing at work. As a result of these discussions, Ben feels that there is nothing about him that she does not know.

Ben's mother enjoys the fact that she and her son both take pleasure in the same sex, and her comments on his lovers have occasionally led to sharp exchanges between them. 'She doesn't restrain herself,' he says. 'Or rather she does restrain herself, but not to the point of shutting up. We have quite a strong bond, when all is said and done.' And when they walk down the street together, she will point out a man that she finds attractive. 'Maybe not,' he will reply. 'She is more of a friend than a mother, I suppose,' is how he summarises the position. 'We have quite a giggle together.'

Why is it, though, that this sort of relaxed intimacy seems so alien to a heterosexual man? What is it about the relationship between a boy and his mother, and the interactions between them which makes the communications between them so tense and fraught? The next chapter will suggest an answer to this question.

CHAPTER TWELVE

Give Me Love, Baby!

A few years ago, my brother fled from an unhappy relationship and a series of career setbacks to take refuge in the attic of our mother's house. One evening, he went to take a swig from a bottle of Polish vodka that he had left in the freezer, and found that it was gone. 'What happened to my vodka?' he asked mother the next morning.

'I drank it,' she replied, without any evident sign of shame.

'You did what?' my brother asked, attempting to show more concern about what he took to be an admission of incipient alcoholism, than anger at the loss of his bottle.

'Well, you drank all my milk,' was her bewildering riposte.

By declaring that she too had needs, and that she now expected from her adult son some return on all the love she had been giving out, my mother hardly said anything strange. Nevertheless, many women do behave as if it would be wrong to treat their full-grown sons as normal human beings. They are mothers, after all, and mothers are not supposed to ask for anything from their babes. In playing along with this idea, they defer to a mothering ideology that bears little relation to reality.

No mother can hope simply to mirror her child's desires;

from the beginning she is a participant in a two-way relationship. She looks to her sons, as to her daughters, for love, warmth and appreciation, and this becomes more and more so as her child matures. Although the Oedipus legend is generally recounted as if Jocasta's feelings and actions played no part in what happened, a mother who waits at the school gate wearing bright red lipstick in order to attract her boy's attention will influence his feelings in a different way from someone who nervously announces when he is ten that she will not kiss or cuddle him anymore because she does not think it right.

This is not about being a good or a bad mum; rather about the fact that a mother is a human being who, by expressing her feelings and her needs, shapes the emotional atmosphere in which her son grows to maturity. However hard she tries not to impose upon her children, a mother simply does not have the power to conceal her feelings. Even the way she holds, feeds and plays with her infant boy contains some sort of a message about what her needs might be. 'The child,' says Chrysoula Worrall, a psychotherapist and mother of boys, 'takes on board mother's needs through osmosis. The words come much later. There is a kind of mutuality of space, and an awful lot of understanding and communication that precedes language. It is a kind of pure feeling that gets communicated. It is not put into words.'

A mother may not want her boy to know the problems she confronts, but if she makes him feel even a little insecure – and she can hardly avoid it – then he will attempt to find out for himself what is going on with her, and to do whatever he can (usually rather little) to avert the outcome that he dreads. As soon as he senses that something is wrong, he will try to work out what is going on. And then he will attempt to make her smile or do something that he thinks will make her happy. Her continued provision of the love that he craves is simply too important a matter for him to let things simply take their course.

'It would be hard,' says psychotherapist Paul van Heeswyck, 'to imagine a relationship in which there were no needs coming from the parent. It would be a question of which ones they were and how significant they were.' The mother who attempts to convey that she is not needy will often be experienced as having a strong need not to be needed. For the boy who senses that his mother is in trouble, her attitude of attempted concealment is a form of rejection. He wants to feel that he can be of use, because doing something about his mother's requirements provides him with reassurance of some sort that he has the capacity to make her stay around for him.

When Melissa's husband walked out on her, she tried not to impose upon her sons the sense that they were responsible for propping her up. 'I did not,' she remarks, 'ever want them to feel that I had stopped them doing or being what they wanted to because they were responsible for my emotional happiness.' Because of this, she never told her boys what she felt about their father: that she hated and loathed him for what he had done. She tried not to undermine their allegiance to him, fearing that, if she did, they might one day come to hate her for poisoning the relationship with their dad. She realises now how her dishonest insistence that she had no need of them drove them both to the other side of the Atlantic so that they could be near their dad, who made a more overt display of his neediness.

The job of parenting tends to bring out in most mothers a powerful awareness of how needy they are. Partly, this is because the child's demandingness revives many of her own feelings from infancy. It is also that suddenly life is turned upside down: many things that were possible once are possible no more. A mother is stuck with a bawling infant who demands her attention all the time, wakes her at all hours, so that often she ends up feeling like a zombie, continuously tired, resentful about the demands now being placed upon her. 'I had stopped being a woman, I had just become a machine,' Jana recalls. 'I was being used, constantly giving, giving, giving and getting nothing back in return.'

In the 'ideal' model put forward by child psychiatrist Donald Winnicott, it is the father's function to soak up these emotions and deflect them from the child. But the father may become ill or find a job that takes him often abroad. Or he may shirk his responsibilities, either because he never expected to be involved, or because he cannot cope with the feelings provoked in him by an infant, or because he just does not have the emotional capacity to understand what his partner is going through. 'I was not being appreciated for what I was doing,' Jana recalls. 'That appreciation should have come from a husband, but it didn't.' In this way, the boy's father becomes part of the problem to which he is supposed to be the solution.

Whatever the reason for his father's absence, there is a strong likelihood that the mother in such a situation will at some point turn towards her son, and ask him to perform the function of a much older man. 'This wife,' says feminist psychoanalyst Nancy Chodorow of the mother whose husband fails to support her, 'is likely to turn her affection and interest to the next obvious male – her son – and to become particularly seductive toward him.'[1]

The writer Elias Canetti, whose autobiography describes how an overwhelming love for mother can be transformed into angry hate, was seven when his father died and, as the eldest son, he was appointed to look after his mother by sleeping in his parents' bed. Lying there, he would pretend he was asleep while she wept. But when she went to stand at the window, his fear that she was about to leap out caused him to jump up, put his arms around her and hold on tight. 'I felt her body yield,' he later wrote, 'when the tension waned, and she turned to me from the despair of her decision. She pressed my head to her body and sobbed louder.'[2] It is common for sons whose fathers have disappeared to feel that they must shower mother with anxious love so as to ensure that she stays around to take care of them.

In less extreme circumstances, a son may feel burdened simply because his mother talks to him about the problems in her life and the difficulties that confront her. Sasha, who says the biggest fear in her life is that her children will stop loving her, took advantage of the daily drive to and from school to tell her son just what she was going through. 'We were very good friends,' she says. 'I off-loaded a hell of a lot on to him. I thought it was good that I should talk to him, since my mother never spoke to me. He must have taken on a hell of a lot of junk. I was always so angry and so hurt. At the time, it was the only way I could cope.' Her son may have felt as Nick did when his mother expressed to him all she felt about having to nurse her husband through fifteen years of illness. 'I can remember,' he says, 'her asking me all sorts of questions, and really I hadn't got a clue.'

For the boy, his mother's confiding to him the state of her feelings is generally experienced as a call for help. I recall that, when I was growing up, I often used to feel that my mother needed my support. She had married a man, my father, who could not begin to satisfy her need for love. Feeling overwhelmed by the demands she tossed at him, he made the situation steadily worse by withdrawing from family responsibilities, forsaking his wife and children for scientific research, music and other women. In thus repeating for my mother the experience of parents who were always putting 'important' work before the needs of their two daughters, he triggered her deepest misery.

Unable to deal with her sense of being abandoned once again, my mother did not try very hard to conceal her despair. I remember her taking me to church one Sunday morning, and making some mysterious remark about how she hoped to feel 'better' afterwards. When we came home, it was soon clear that the hoped-for religious magic had not worked. At lunch-time, my mother emitted a low moan which went on, without any serious interruption that I can now recall, until late in the night. Unable to cope, my father retreated into his study, making us all feel that the scientific paper he was writing mattered much more to him than his four children did. After we should all long ago have been asleep, our mother was lying on the stairs, her face red with despair and weeping, willing my father to come out and talk to her. But when he finally did emerge, he seemed helpless either to provide comfort or to reach out in any way to his deeply-confused children.

I longed to improve the situation between my parents, but I did not really know what else I could do. Eventually I just gave up and locked myself away in my room, much as my father used to do, and began to long for the day when I could finally escape this emotional cauldron. When he was thirteen, my brother had an even more intense and enduring confrontation with mother's neediness. My father quit the house for good within a few weeks of my own departure for the Middle East, and my brother was left as the only male in the house. In this capacity, he was called upon to carry the brunt of our two sisters' anger with men, and to provide emotional support to a mother who was now tearful, distraught and in the early stages of a breakdown. 'There she was,' he recalls now, 'wailing and asking me to make things better. That's what I wanted to do. I wanted mummy to stop crying, to be better again. I tried to fulfil the male role, which I couldn't really do.'

Girls too want their mothers to stop crying, to come out of their depressions, to talk honestly and openly about what they are going through, but they receive different messages from their brothers. When a mother is not getting what she needs from her husband, she tends to say to her boy, or is felt to be saying, that the hurt she feels is the fault of men, that men are not strong enough or responsive enough to make her feel good about herself. As she talks about these things, she conveys to him the hope that he will be able to do what no man has ever been able to do before: to make her happy, to make things easy for her. And for as long as her love is important to him, he is hardly likely to refuse the challenge outright.

Albert cannot remember a time when he did not want to make things better for his mother. Growing up in the East End of London during the 1930s, he watched her burn old boots and other rubbish to heat the water for the daily wash. He recalls days when there was nothing to eat but bread and jam. But most vividly of all, he remembers those Saturdays when his carpenter father took his weekly wages down to the pub. At closing time, Albert and his two brothers would hide under the bed-clothes, waiting to hear the sound of doors being broken, windows being smashed and bedroom furniture being flung out onto the streets, which was all mere preparation for the weekly row that would then blow up between his mother and his father. 'The men had a hard life,' Albert says, 'but the women had it ten times harder.'

Having heard his father's threats of murder coming from downstairs, Albert felt enormous sympathy for his defenceless mother, and he would express this in different ways as he grew older. When only a small boy, he would scrub the kitchen floor and do the washing-up. After leaving school at fourteen to go and work as a bricklayer, he would hand over the greater part of his wages to his mother, while starting to stand up for her against his father. And when he was in his mid-twenties, just back from fighting in Italy with the British army, he finally ejected his father from the house so as to relieve his mother of her trouble.

Albert had come home to discover that his father was not only drinking as much as ever, but had taken up with another woman. Older, stronger and more confident of his powers than he had previously been, he tracked his father down to the pub where he was carousing. The time had come, he felt, for a showdown. 'If this don't stop,' he said to his father, 'you can get out.'

'Don't you tell me to get out of my own house,' Albert's father replied, while trying to conceal the presence of his mistress alongside him.

'It ain't your house as far as I'm concerned,' Albert countered. 'Either pack it up now and lead a decent life or get out and lead the life you want to lead.'

Albert's father came home that night with a promise to reform. 'You don't know anything,' he declared defiantly to his son. It was his last stand: he moved in with the other woman shortly afterwards. 'He must have realised,' says Albert, 'that I was bigger than him by then.'

The pressure on Albert to do something about his mother's situation was powerful even though never directly expressed. She had not asked him to solve the problem of his father's violence, nor had they discussed together what strategies might bring about the desired end, but she often turned to him for protection and support. 'Where are you going?' she would ask him as he went to the door on a Saturday night, 'so that I know where to find you if he starts.' Albert was clearly right to deduce that his mother would welcome liberation from her marriage to a drunken philanderer.

There are many things that mothers may ask their sons to do for them: to listen to their secrets; to take a stand against their husbands; to help provide solutions to their financial problems; to cuddle them, embrace them, fondle them and provide consolation for the cruelties inflicted by lovers, landlords or employers. She may also want him to soak up her frustration about her relative lack of success in life, or make her feel better about her own educational limitations by doing well at school. 'Some parents,' Bruno Bettelheim once wrote, 'unconsciously view their child so much as part of themselves that they cannot imagine that what gives them pleasure, such as academic prowess, could have a very different effect on their child.'[3]

The consequences of a mother's turning to her son need

not be totally negative. Albert says that the battles which he undertook on his mother's behalf taught him to despise violence, to respect women and to confront every situation with an easy-going smile. By teaching her son that she experiences pain as well as happiness, a mother reveals that she is a woman too, not just a slave standing by to service his needs. By forcing him to react to her demands, she may help a son to form his own goals and values. And the mother who drives her son to achieve academically and make up for what she sees as her own intellectual deficiencies, may imbue him with a love of learning that enriches his whole life. In general, by asking her boy to do things for her, a mother may be seen as acknowledging that he is no longer a helpless baby, that he has potential of his own. But he needs then to move on from his mother's project for him, and to find out what he really wants for himself, if he is ever to feel truly content with what he is doing and who he is.

It is when a mother asks of her son something that he cannot possibly achieve, because he is too weak or too immature, and then does not acknowledge how he is being affected by his failure, even expresses anger at his inability to meet her needs, that problems arise. While Albert clearly looks back with enormous pride at his achievement in ejecting a vicious father from the family home, many sons have found themselves completely helpless in such situations. Bryan remembers an occasion when he was thirteen and his mother was involved in a row with his sozzled father, who sat on the bottom of the stairs with a bottle of rum between his knees, declaring that he was about to drive away. Bryan's mother thrust the car keys into her son's hands and pleaded with him to stop his father going out. 'It felt really bizarre and intensely stressful,' he recalls. 'Suddenly I was this little kiddie in charge of an adult situation. I remember thinking that he was going to whack me. I felt very confused about it.'

And if it is hard to be the third party in a conflict between parents, it is even more difficult to experience oneself being asked by mother to deal with emotional problems that one cannot begin to understand. The son knows he is being asked for something that he cannot deliver. Because he is unable to relieve the neediness, he feels held by it. It worries him, troubles him and develops into a recurring obsession. Since he cannot anticipate the eventual consequences of his failure, he becomes anxious. Because he seems so inadequate, he falls all too easily into despair. He may feel guilty too that he cannot match up to his mother's hopes, while also being angry that his mother dumps so much upon him.

It would be much easier for the boy if he knew that his father was needy too, so that he felt less alone in his engagement with mother, but whatever it is that dad might be feeling is usually only revealed in confusing bursts, through an occasional alcoholic storm, an outburst of violence or a protracted sulk. My father, for example, was undoubtedly just as miserable as my mother, if not more so, but he would take his unhappiness away to the pub, his laboratory or a lover's bedroom, whereas my mother was always with us, spreading quiet panic by telling us how she would like to go to sleep and never wake up. It was partly because she was stuck with us that she was so unhappy, and because we were stuck with her that we knew so much about that unhappiness.

What so many men never learn, because their fathers do not tell them, is that everyone is needy to some degree. Since their fathers are so often not around to listen, their sons are not enabled properly to explore their own neediness. And because they are often exposed to so much emotional pressure from their mothers, of a sort that they do not have the physical or emotional resources to handle, they develop a distorted attitude to women. Having understood the message from mother as a summons to produce a satisfactory response and then having miserably failed to do so, they become convinced that all women are impossibly needy, that they are inadequate to meet these needs, that there is literally nothing they can do. They cannot respond to a woman's call because they lack real confidence in their ability to provide an adequate response. Confronted by the demands of women, they experience feelings of confusion, anger and bewilderment, then withdraw to a safe place.

Since men cannot acknowledge these feelings of inadequacy, and women are bewildered by the experience of men running away from *their* declarations of need, there exists no common understanding between men and women over this issue. Every complaint from a woman is experienced by the man as an impossible, hysterical demand. Each failure by a man to rise to the occasion is seen by the woman as a sure sign of his inability to love her.

When I, like my brother, had gone to live in my mother's house for a second time, a former girlfriend phoned me, expressed her concern and suggested that we meet for dinner. During the meal she became increasingly vexed by my account of what I was doing to pay off substantial debts. Finally, she stared intently at me, took a long drag on her cigarette and bellowed in a voice that was loud enough to embarrass all the other restaurant diners, 'You have got to stop sucking on your mother's tit.' A few weeks later, I received from her a Christmas card that showed a little boy looking out of a window at Raymond Briggs's *Snowman*.

Her words summarised all the problems that there had always been in our relationship. It was quite impossible for her to accept that any man might be needy, dependent and unable to support himself, even temporarily. Since all the men she had ever known, from her father onwards, had been inadequate to deal with her needs, she longed to find a man who could. She was drawn to men who reminded her of her father, tried to change them, then ranted at them because they failed. And although she talked about some men she had known who were different, they were always the ones who had left her rather speedily, or to whom she had been only one of many. Throughout our stormy three-year relationship, she expressed in forceful terms her demand that I should 'take care' of her. When I asked what more she wanted me to offer than I was already providing, she would stomp off in a huff, as if I was supposed to understand the needs that she hardly comprehended herself, and to respond effectively to them. Nothing I did was ever enough, and my attempts were greeted with a series of increasingly hysterical aspersions upon my masculinity.

Only gradually did I come to realise that I was being asked to do the impossible, to heal the pain left behind by my girlfriend's unsatisfactory relationship with her father and with other men. Locked to her by compulsive sexual desire, provoked by her challenge that I should prove myself in her eyes, I hung around, trying to deliver at least some of what she was requesting, until her anger became too much to bear. The experiences I had with my own mother convinced me that I should stay, because that is what I thought men were supposed to do, but they had also left me with no conviction that I could succeed in meeting the needs of this needy woman.

In comparison with their distant fathers, most boys experience their mothers as highly emotional, whether depressed, moody or ranting, and this comes to shape their views both of women and of their own position in relation to women. They see female outpourings as a threat to their safety and a challenge to their competence. Never offered any encouragement from father, they are not given a chance to express what they feel. 'The horrible thing,' one merchant banker said to me of his mother's outlook on the world, 'is that there is no framework, no guidance, no knowledge of what she wants. There's no way you can help her. She won't allow you to help her. There is absolutely zero structure. I want a clearer, fairer world which has proper guidelines, rather than just the emotional whims of a particular human being.'

In the next chapter, I will look at how men's experience of their mother's emotional openness leads to the development of their own emotional block and all the other ills of masculinity.

CHAPTER THIRTEEN

Emotional Block

It still bewilders me when male friends withdraw into sullen silence because something has been asked of them by their partners. They will stomp off upstairs, or withdraw into a side room and put on some music, even in the middle of their own dinner parties, clearly in pain or angry about something, but with no way to express their feelings. It is as if they do not know what has been stirred up in them by the request that has been made, or that they believe nobody would listen if they were to speak: this despite the fact that women will have begged them many times to say everything that they feel. In the end, these men cannot speak because they do not have any grasp of what they want to say: they do not understand their own desire.

The family environment in which most men grow to maturity does not encourage them to understand their own emotions. In those early years when mother is all and everything to him, the little boy can take to her any graze on his knee or fluttering of anxiety, but the steady decline in intimacy between a boy and his mother destroys this sense of emotional ease. As he experiences things being asked of him, he starts to cut himself off from her, to conceal what he is feeling. 'The silence that mothers so often encounter as their sons enter the outside world,' writes journalist Angela Phillips in her book *The Problem with Boys*, 'is bound up with their need to be separate. To find a life for themselves. To discover what it means to be male.'[1] His mother's expectation that he, being a boy, will behave in this sort of way gives her little incentive to try and penetrate the wall that has been put up.

The result is that boys grow up trying to tackle problems of ever greater emotional sophistication in the company of a mother in whom they are steadily less willing to confide, and who is mostly less and less capable of hearing what they try to say. This conspiracy of silence is all too rarely broken by a father's (useful) intervention; for few men are willing to sit down and seriously listen to what their sons deeply feel. The boy picks up a sense that nobody is interested, and that therefore there is no point in talking. These are problems not admitting of a solution; therefore they should be hidden, never discussed or raised. He must present the best possible face to the world and get on with it. While girls may find themselves in a similar situation, they learn something from the relative emotional fluency of their mothers. They have the opportunity to identify with a woman who can be open about her feelings, and who feels a sense of affiliation to her daughter.

Most mothers want to believe that they stand ever-ready to take on the woes, hopes and fears that their children bring up, but a whole host of factors can block their eyes and ears. The woman juggling work and domestic commitments generally has little time left over to attend seriously to the needs of someone else, and it is natural for someone whose every day is filled with chores, duties and activities to work on the assumption that everything is okay until, that is, she is told that her boy is disrupting the class, shoplifting from the local department store or beating up small children. And she may just assume that childish problems are likely to be resolved 'naturally' by the passage of time.

She can also justify to herself almost anything that her son does by declaring that boys will be boys. She may believe that big boys should not cry. She may feel that a male child must learn to endure on his own the rigours of life, so that he can be 'toughened' up. She may also resist hearing him because she feels that she is not able to understand the feelings of someone who belongs to a different sex from herself, or because she feels resentment against men, or because she dislikes seeing feminine 'weakness' mirrored in her boy, whom she hopes will eventually come to protect her. Since she wants men around who are different from her, available for her to lean on, she can easily accept that her boy does not have the quality of emotional openness.

When Dorothy looks back upon the childhood of her son Giles, she feels that there were all too many occasions when she failed to tune into his pain and distress, to come forward and reassure him that somebody cared for him and was willing to listen to whatever he wanted to tell her, whatever it was that he felt. She had wanted to be the sort of maternal figure who was always there for her children, ready with a cake when they came home from school, actively involved in their drawing, reading and homework, altogether very different from her own career-driven mother. But she always found it much harder to make a connection to her son than to her daughters. She recalls that, if Giles ever teased his baby sister, she would grab him by the shirt, shake him and fling him onto the bed, shrieking 'Leave her alone!'

When Dorothy's husband took the family to Paris, the six-year-old Giles was put into a French-speaking school which he hated, so much so that his mother had to drag him onto the bus each morning, and there encourage the driver to shut the doors quickly so that Giles did not have a chance to jump off. He would come home in tears, and receive a lecture from his mother about how, if he really needed to cry when he was at school, he should go into the toilet to do it. 'I did that with the best will in the world,' Dorothy says, recognising now that he took this as meaning he should hide his tears from everyone, including her.

One evening, Dorothy went to collect her son. He descended from the bus looking green, to a chorus of jeers from those boys who were left behind. It emerged that when, in the morning, Giles had asked a teacher if he could go to the toilet, she had refused permission. Unable to control himself, Giles had walked around all day with his trousers full of shit. As Dorothy forced her son to talk about what had happened, she realised for the first time how she had blocked from her own mind any awareness of Giles's true feelings about his school. 'I used to feel terrible walking away from the bus,' she says, 'but then I would shut it out. I felt he had to go to school.' Despite these doubts, the next morning Dorothy took her boy to the bus stop, gave him a big hug and pushed him back onto the bus.

Shortly afterwards, though, Dorothy did tell her husband that they must go back to London, so that Giles could settle back into life at an English school. He seemed to become happier, until he reached his early teens and felt the effect of his father's 'interest' in his school work. These interventions seemed to be motivated more by jealousy than genuine concern. Dorothy, feeling that an art school training did not entitle her to challenge the highly-educated son of a university Dean, shut her eyes and ears as her husband, who had not wanted children and never made much effort to establish a connection with the boy, began throwing books at their son, calling him names and beating him around the head. 'It was just too awful,' she says. But she felt unable to intervene or to let Giles know that she sympathised with him over the treatment he was receiving from his bully of a father. She regarded her son's suffering as a necessary part of his development. 'I've never really thought,' she says to me, 'about how it must have been for Giles, not having an ally in the house.'

Passing through adolescence with a father who seemed to hate him and a mother who stood apart from 'men's business', Giles had no one to whom he could express his feelings. He turned to drugs in the hope that they would numb his pain, and pushed his emotions yet more deeply down into his psyche. He started smoking cannabis when he was twelve, and was soon lighting up in the morning to get himself out of bed. At the first possible opportunity, Giles blew out his studies and went off to India where he was arrested for possessing heroin and had to spend three months in prison before his mother could arrange for his release. He later went to Thailand, where a road accident deprived him of his one potential escape hatch, his job as a cycle messenger. 'He really has gone downhill fast from there,' his mother says.

Giles is now 27, and a heroin addict living in a squat. He spends most of his days lying curled up on a sofa watching television, with his arms above his head. The last time his mother saw him, he looked like the sort of tramp who sleeps in London doorways; unwashed, with a filthy, matted bundle of hair upon his head. When she tried talking to him, he just grunted and left the house. Dorothy wants to help her son, to prove to him that she loves him and cares about him, but she still does not know how to go about it. 'What I would like to do,' she says, 'is to shut myself up in a room with him, sit him there, chained up, so that he could not escape from it, and get him to open up. I would really like to know what Giles's true feelings are.' And yet this urge to be her son's guardian angel is still restrained by the sense that it would be wrong to interfere. 'This is his path,' she says, 'and it is up to him to deal with it.'

Most mothers have been in situations where they started to wonder why the boy who once seemed so open now slouches around the house looking glum, unwilling to inform her that he is being bullied at school, or that he is failing to understand maths. 'I find that having a conversation with James,' remarks Sheila of her son, 'is like getting blood out of a stone. It takes a while to get him to tell me anything.' Confronted by their sons' long silences and stony stares, many point at the expectations that society has of its men, as communicated to them by their schoolteachers, their fathers and their peers, thus disclaiming any (albeit shared) responsibility for the situation.

It would be far more honest to admit that the communications coming from their boys had not been clear, that it takes a special kind of attentiveness to tune into the confused and muddled feelings that a child has, and that it is difficult to do that when the soup is boiling over, the television is on or granny is dying. 'We should not expect our children,' Bruno Bettelheim once wrote, 'to be able to tell us what they feel deeply about, or what is going on in their inner selves, particularly since so much of it is not accessible to their conscious minds and they are therefore unable to articulate it.'[2]

A boy may not recognise that his mother would be willing to hear his feelings and his troubles if only he were to approach her in the right way. What he mostly sees is her emotional neediness, which makes him think that she should not be burdened with his (insignificant) difficulties and experiences: he must cope on his own. She may occupy so much emotional space that he forms the view there is nowhere left in which he can insert his feelings. He may conclude from her volubility that it is less important for him to articulate his own emotions than to let his mother voice hers. Lacking her emotional fluency, he blocks his inner world and does not tell her that he is being victimised, or having trouble with his work, or feeling confused about the blood-spattered news bulletins that he sees.

'My own needs were pretty secondary to the needs of the situation,' says Henry about the experience of growing up with an unstable father and a highly-strung mother. 'You had to compensate to make life easier for her, because she was under pressure. I learned not to talk about this or that. The toughness that went into coping meant that there was a certain lack of emotional ease.' Jeremy had a mother whose unhappiness put him always on his guard. When he was seven, a close school-friend died from kidney failure. Having received the news at school assembly in the morning, he spent the day wondering how he would tell his mum. He knew she would be upset, would probably break down and cry, and he could not bring himself to cause her such distress. For two days, he kept the news to himself, until finally he was forced to reveal it by his mother's inquiry about his friend's health. Her ensuing lamentations left him, as he had feared, with no space in which to experience his own pain and grief, but with a much more acute awareness of his mother's unhappiness. The fact that his mother was invited to the funeral, and he was not, confirmed his sense that her response was more important than his own.

Because he attempts to rise to his mother's challenge, to summon up the emotional strength that her neediness seems to require, the son comes to the view that mother should not be troubled with his problems. In setting out to defend, protect or comfort her, he learns that it is her role to unload emotionally, his to respond practically. He tries to make things better, and when the consequence of his mission is failure, as it all too often is, the existing problems of communication are compounded by his feelings of guilt, shame and remorse.

When Bernard, now a schoolteacher in his mid-forties, came to speak with me, he said very firmly that he did not want anything to appear in print which his mother might identify as being about her and find hurtful. It soon became clear that he was anxious not so much to protect his mother, but to insulate himself against her, and that he had been doing this all his life. 'I can keep her sweet,' he said. 'I do not think that there is anything to be gained by upsetting her.'

Bernard has always tried to ensure that nothing he said or did would stoke his mother's wrath or increase her sense of unhappiness. This defensive drive is so strong because he never quite worked out why she was so angry, short-tempered and erratic in her behaviour, and yet it seems that nothing he did ever seemed to work in holding back his mother's rage.

'We were always terrified of my mother,' Bernard recalls, 'Even today, if she raises her voice in a certain way, I will instinctively cower.' There was one occasion when Bernard felt unjustly rebuked for failing to clean the kitchen floor. 'Why didn't *you* do it?' he replied. This provoked her into grabbing the nearest available implement, which was a carving knife, and plunging it into his leg. He staunched his wound and left the house for a day. When he came back, hoping that, in a calmer mood, she might apologise for what she had done, she only blamed him for having made her so angry.

Bernard and his three sisters were given reason to believe that they were at least partially responsible for their mother's distress. 'I hate children,' she would say. And when her little ones quivered their chins, pouted their lips and looked teary-eyed, she would try to cheer them up a little, asserting, 'Oh, you're my children, that's different.' Such reassurance was not enough to remove from Bernard the impression that his existence and actions had provoked the remark. He did what he could to make his mother feel better, becoming a boy who never made any demands, in contrast to his sisters' noisy articulation of their needs.

When Bernard's mother told her husband that she could no longer bear to live with him, he suggested to his son that one way of blocking the divorce might be for him to reveal to the court that mummy and daddy still occasionally shared a bed. In his eight-year-old innocence, Bernard announced this strategy for marital reconciliation to his mother. Instead of acknowledging her son's quite natural desire that his parents should stay together, and quietly explaining to him that this would be impossible, she started to scream at him. 'Do you really want mummy to be unhappy and miserable?' was the gist of what she said.

Bernard feels that the effect of his mother never having acknowledged his feelings, but creating instead a situation in which he had to repress all his anger against her, has been to make it impossible for him to express any emotion at all.

He remembers an evening when he was about eleven. He had come home to mow the lawn, but gave up after the machine's blades became entangled in some string. When his mother came home to find the lawn-mower sitting on the half-cut swathe and her son watching his favourite television programme, she started to shout at him. His excuse was shrugged off with the assertion that it was his fault if there was string lying on the grass. Ordered to bed without any supper, Bernard started to cry. She told him that tears were for children. From that day on, he says, he has only been able to weep when he was both very drunk and extremely unhappy.

The problem for a boy like Bernard is that his mother stirs up extraordinarily powerful emotions – of love and of hate – and he has no one to whom he can express these feelings apart from the person who aroused them. He also does not have enough experience upon which to assess what the effect of doing this might be. Would his mother perhaps reject him, hit him and refuse to feed him, clothe him or love him anymore? He may make a few forays into the area of self-expression and find enough evidence in the cross retorts he receives that this is not a very wise course to take. He may try talking to his father, only to find that he does not want to listen, or that he automatically takes his wife's point of view, because that seems like the most diplomatic option. Neither parent seems willing to acknowledge that their son needs to express exactly what he feels, so that these emotions can lose some of their violent force and become subject to rational examination.

After furniture mover Terry's mother had walked out and left him, as I described in Chapter Nine, to be followed soon after by his father, he had no one to whom he could express his distress and anger. When two years later his mother came to collect her two boys, the precariousness of the situation made it equally impossible for him to be honest about his feelings, for fear of the harm such openness might wreak.

The result is that even now the only negative emotion he can volunteer towards his mother is a slight sense of 'resentment'.

Terry's deeper feelings are perhaps suggested by the sense of horror with which the new home is still associated in his mind. He describes the place as being full of vermin, so that he would go to bed at night, hear the mice running between the walls and think that they were after him. His mother had also developed a heart condition, possibly as a result of having another child, which made it impossible for her to walk very far. This was all the pretext that Terry needed for channelling his anger towards his mother's new man. 'I always blamed him,' he says. 'I used to think if she hadn't've left my dad, she wouldn't have this condition.'

Terry was never able to make peace with his mother's fourth husband. Whenever he was in a football match with his stepfather, he would make sure he was on the opposing side so that he could kick him in the shins. On one occasion when this usurper said something over dinner which upset their mother, Terry and his brother threw their food on the floor and faced him, saying, 'You shouldn't do that to my mum. You shouldn't even be with my mum.' But what did Terry feel about the way his mother had behaved? By being angry with his stepfather, he could avoid facing the feelings that he had about her. That was perhaps why he found himself so confused and strangely distressed when she became more seriously ill, and eventually died.

After his mother had gone into hospital for an operation, Terry could not bring himself to go and see her, because it upset him too much. His reaction was just as extreme when she was re-admitted and judged too frail for further intervention. Cajoled by his sisters, he did eventually visit the hospital, where he was told that her condition was poorly and that she did not have long to live. But he stood forlornly outside the intensive care unit, unable to go inside. 'I couldn't bear,' he says, 'to think of her with tubes and pipes and monitors, nearly dead, just being kept alive by machines and all that.'

When later his mother was lying in a Chapel of Rest, Terry went briefly to see her. 'Did you kiss her?' his brother asked as he came out.

'No,' Terry replied. 'I didn't want to.'

'Why not?' his brother asked.

'Because I like to think of her as she was, not dead.'

'You should have anyway,' his brother insisted.

'What I have done to me is right,' Terry then said, hoping to fend off any further altercations.

While reproaching his stepfather for the process of decay that destroyed his mother, Terry blamed himself too. Had his own hidden anger, he found himself asking, brought about her physical devastation? When he talks about his 'mum' to me, he never makes her sound like a flesh and blood woman. Instead, she is an idealised creature, a woman he longed for while she was away and cherished in fantasy when they were reunited. The force of his feelings meant that he could never resolve the gap between the good mother he sought and the bad mother who had abandoned him. And even now he is deaf to his feelings of anger.

If a boy lacks access to any parent or other adult who can listen attentively to his confusions and anxieties, he cannot hope to bring them under control. Unable to know his emotions, he will not grow in understanding of himself, nor develop the sort of maturity that is the essential basis for any truly mutual relationship. Just occasionally the feelings will find a way to struggle through. Sometimes, for example, the experience of falling in love takes a man back to his early years of openness sufficiently to allow disclosure. But as the love becomes more developed, as the old fears and anxieties are stirred, reminding him of the way his mother challenged him and did not listen, all too often the boy who has become a man clams up again. Instead of exposing what he feels, he hides his emotions so deep that not even a partner begging him to talk can bring forth any sort of response. The next chapter looks at the Trad Man, who suffers acutely from this failing.

CHAPTER FOURTEEN

Trad Men

The best place to study Trad Men is at the sort of parties which parents throw for other parents, generally starting at noon on a summer Sunday. Hamburgers and pieces of chicken grill on the barbecue that glows against the garden wall. Other guests drink beer, wine or orange juice. And as the gathering thickens, the men split off from the women and the world of children is divided from the realm of men. While the men huddle and talk about politics, the firm or football, the women take responsibility for the kids who run around the garden and attack each other. Once in a while, one of these little ones will be carried across the divide and thrust into the arms of its father, or a man will move away with a slight air of reluctance to perform some parenting chore, but generally the Trad Man's rule will be upheld: even in a social situation where both parents are there on equal terms, it is women who must supervise, discipline and feed the children.

It is often suggested that the creation of a working environment in which men and women had equal opportunities to look after the children would change these men. But the sight of the two sexes dividing up their responsibilities in this way always makes me wonder: is there not something unchangeable about the way in which these fathers abdicate emotional and childcare responsibilities to their wives, something that can never be shifted simply by persuading generations of men to be more relaxed about their work commitments?

It is not, of course, that there is anything wrong with men coming together to enjoy each other's company, drink lots of beer, talk dirty and then discuss the future of the government, but their reluctance to do the nurturing, emotional, relating things as well suggests that something is being pushed away into the nether regions of their psyches. Corinna can easily talk with her girlfriend about politics between chatter about what their mutual friends and acquaintances are getting up to in the bedroom, but her husband never seems to discuss anything personal with anyone. 'Is your colleague still having an affair?' his wife will ask. 'I don't know', he will reply. 'Is your friend happily married?' 'What's it got to do with me?' I don't know and I don't care is the message she receives.

The Trad Man is very far from being any kind of hypocritical monster. He respects the gender divide but he does not need to guard it with the same totalitarian intensity as the Chauvinist. He will happily let his wife go out to work, make decisions about investments and hold on to the channel-zapper in the evenings. Once in a while he will do some work around the house: he might iron the clothes, put some bleach down the toilet and scrub the floor. He is an attentive lover who would never hit his wife. When he does get angry, as he quite often does, he is more likely to stomp off upstairs than vent his feelings openly. He tends to remember birthdays and anniversaries. He is affectionate and supportive, liking few things better than to sit down over a bottle of wine and talk to his wife about what has been going on in her day. He also has a strong sense of duty towards his mother, to whom he would seldom say a cross word.

He enjoys feeling involved in bringing up his children and being called father. He gets a thrill from occasionally helping out with his children's homework. He will take them to their football matches, and organise outings to theme parks, fairgrounds and museums. And he feels good when he is called in to deal with the 'big issues' around children: to be briefed by the headmaster, the policeman or the social worker about what his son or daughter has been doing in their spare time.

But suggest to him that he let his wife's job take priority for more than an occasional fortnight, and he is likely to feel distinctly uncomfortable; for the thought of having to plan his children's timetables and organise their welfare cuts too deeply into his sense of the masculine role. He is willing to re-negotiate the sexual contract, but always within limits. He feels secure with the existing arrangements, and does not want them to be changed in any way. He sees the maintenance of some degree of segregation as not only 'natural' but very much necessary.

When you meet a Trad Man, it is likely that he will impress by the air of quiet confidence that he gives off. He may have the sort of physique that comes from weekly games of squash or a regular run around a track. He presents himself as a man who has never found life particularly difficult, nor does he show any sign of serious dissatisfaction with his lot. You might envy him for his sense of being at ease with himself. You might also wonder what he is trying to hide.

More perhaps than any other type of man, the Trad Man takes his style from his parents. Having seen the arrangement work well enough for them, he has never been unhappy enough to contemplate change. He will expect his wife to do as his mother did, fulfilling her responsibilities in the kitchen and the cleaning cupboard, while he carries out his in the boardroom or on the shop-floor. As long as he provides solidity, she offers spontaneity and fluidity. Wherever he is deficient, she will provide, and vice versa.

For David, a businessman in his early forties, the contrast between his parents was marked. His father was a solitary man who came to know the neighbours only through his wife, and whose favourite leisure-time activities were walking the dog or pottering around the garden. He worked hard, though, to build up his business and to bring in the funds required to support a family. David's mother, by contrast, was gregarious and outgoing, a keen tennis player and later a leading light in the bowls club. David's early memories are of his mother as a housewife who shopped, cooked, put up the ironing board and hung out the washing. Having given up the secretarial business that she ran upon becoming pregnant, she contented herself thereafter with working for various voluntary organisations, and keeping the books for her husband.

The differences between husband and wife were quickly obvious when I went to talk with David's mother at her home beside the sea. The man of the house chose to sit in on her interview, and made a series of interjections that showed how difficult he found it to cope with the emotional issues that his wife was cheerfully discussing. 'So there you are,' he said when the tape-recorder had only been running for five minutes. 'What questions do you want to ask?' He seemed to find the pace so slow and the questions so irritating that I several times wondered if he was planning to boot me out of the door. Occasionally, he expressed his feelings by making trumpet-blowing noises and tapping the arm of his chair. 'Anyway,' he said defensively at one point. 'What are you getting at? We always helped him in any way we could.' I did not pick up the impression of a man much inclined to listen to what his wife might be saying.

David's mother could rear a Trad Man because she felt reasonably contented with her lot. She was never motivated to exclaim against the burden that her children placed upon her, nor to express any complaints and anxieties to them. She seemed happy to act as a 'good transport system', taking her two sons to football matches and other sporting fixtures. She accepted them more or less as they were, neither pressing them to perform at an exceptionally high level, nor requiring them to be angels. When David's school performance slipped, for example, she encouraged him to do better, but did not convey to him that she was anxious about what was happening. 'Although,' he says, 'the error of my ways was pointed out, I was never condemned.' Nor was there any sort of angry interchange when he came back rolling drunk from an end-of-cast party. 'We were very upset,' his mother says, 'but we did not blame him.'

The Trad Boy absorbs an emotional atmosphere that is never ruffled: the expression of strong feelings is discouraged, and his mother conveys the message that, if he is to become a man like his father, then he must learn to dull his sensitivity and not reveal to her or to anyone else his day-to-day difficulties. She makes him aware that she is not available to him in the way that she might be to a daughter. He is, after all, of a different sex to her.

David's mother recalls a period when her son gave off every indication that he was unhappy. 'Is everything all right?' she would tentatively ask him, clearly seeking for reassurance that it was.

'Yes,' he would dishonestly reply, and say nothing more. One day, though, she was at a coffee morning when another parent commented on the fact that David was having a bad time at school.

'Is he?' she replied. The other parent then revealed that her son was being quite seriously bullied.

'He is big enough to stand up for himself,' David's mother said, as if to justify her ignorance and apparent lack of concern.

'I think it has got a bit beyond that,' the other parent replied.

Feeling worried, David's mother made contact with the headmaster at his school, but she never raised the matter directly with her son. Indeed, she felt proud of him for being so determined to deal with the matter on his own. 'I respected him,' she says, 'for being the sort of boy who does not tell tales.'

Experiencing no strong pressures from his mother, nor any serious fluctuation in maternal love, the Trad Man charts a course through life that is characterised by application and determination rather than passion and intensity. Never having been particularly dissatisfied with what his mother had to offer, he is not in any particular hurry to transfer his affections elsewhere, even though he is happy with the thought that he might one day marry. 'Having a girlfriend,' David says, 'was not fundamentally an important thing.' Even when he was in his mid-twenties, he followed the line laid down by his parents, that it was best to sort out the practical details of his life before becoming seriously involved with a woman.

When the Trad Man does eventually establish a family, he sets out to re-establish the sort of arrangements that he knew as a child, taking a conscientious attitude to the responsibilities he has for his wife, his children and his parents, but never establishing, or really looking for, any close connection to them. He is the sort of son that many a mother says she would like to have produced, and many a wife thinks she would prefer to the irresponsible scallywags she does in fact put up with. The wife of a Trad Man is often told that she is lucky to have such a fine husband, so that she often asks herself if she is simply greedy when driven to complain that something is missing.

Most of the Trad Men I tried to interview told me that I would be wasting my time, since they had nothing to say. It was only as a result of badgering from their wives that one or two were brought round to the idea. This may have been why, when David's wife greeted me at the door, her warm smile hinted at the existence of some sort of conspiracy between us. She led me into the kitchen where her husband was fingering his way through a box of documents that related to the family tax affairs. As she brewed up a cup of coffee for us both, I started trying to break through David's diffidence, the sense he gave off that he was an unwilling victim whom I was leading towards the abattoir. Whereas his wife's warmth drew me towards her, he froze me out. And yet I picked up from her an air of fragility, so that I worried about the possibility that a casual remark from me might be misinterpreted, causing her to scurry away hurt. I wondered whether this was why she married a man who did not look as if he would ever say an unkind thing or lash out in fury, even though it now frustrated her that he did not open up to her more or reveal something about his feelings.

There is not a man in this book who does not have some sort of problem with intimacy, but the syndrome is most clearly seen in the case of the Trad Man because it is his most striking flaw. However hard his wife tries to unblock his emotions, nothing seems to work. Something is missing, some part of him has been cut off or never developed. The Trad Man brings to mind Robert Bly's account of modern men. 'You quickly notice the lack of energy in them,' he writes in *Iron John*. 'They are life-preserving but not exactly life-giving.'[1]

The paradox is that the culture for which Bly argues as a remedy for the ills of modern men would seem to be precisely the sort that produces Trad Men. For it is when male and female are treated as distinct categories that men grow up without any understanding of what they feel or any capacity to express emotions to their partners. Because the Trad Man matures in a home where emotional expression was discouraged, the deeper parts of himself remain unknown and uncharted. He cannot open up to his anger, fear and longing because he is terrified of what the consequences would be and doubts whether he would have the strength to deal with them. Needing to keep control over himself, and over his partner, he uses his gender as part of his safety system. He explains his wife's greater contact with her emotions as resulting from the difference between the sexes. He wants to be largely an observer of emotional life, not too much an active participant.

'The minute it gets too close,' says Mary of her husband, 'he backs off. He says that he doesn't like being close to people, exposing himself to people.'

This characteristic of men is often written about as their greatest strength. It is, some have argued, their 'exile' from the world of intimacy that has enabled them to create profitable companies, build grand buildings and develop sophisticated philosophies, but a man cannot really be called strong who knows only one part of himself, and refuses through fear to go really close to another person. Such a man is bound to be grudging in his dispensation of love and affection. He tries hard to pretend that he does not crave the love of women, refusing to acknowledge his desire to be cherished and supported. By upholding the traditional division of sexual responsibility, he can cut off one part of his potential, rendering rigid and limiting what could, if fluid, free him for a relationship of true mutuality. The wife in such relationships has to resign herself to the fact that a Trad Man will always be a Trad Man, and that he will probably never grasp why she sometimes feels so discontented with the arrangement.

CHAPTER FIFTEEN

Lashing Out

'Okay. As long as you're okay. I don't want to phone and interfere.'

Sylvia was stretched out on a long brown sofa, complaining of a bad back, with her thin legs in blue and white polka-dot leggings pointed towards the large television set on which an ancient episode of *Dynasty* was soundlessly passing. She was talking to her 27-year-old son, who had left home a week earlier in order to set up house with his girlfriend. Her words expressed anxiety that the relationship might not endure (he was, in fact, to return home some eight months later.) The conversation's banalities were just what you might expect from a caring mother and a loving son as they talked over the telephone.

I was only half-listening though; for Julian's call enabled me to look again at the newspaper article that Sylvia had brought to my attention, in which a British psychotherapist put forward the argument of his new book, that men hate women, and that their feelings flow inevitably from the relationships that they have with their mothers. 'Men exist in a state of perpetual enmity towards women which they express overtly and covertly, by controlling and dominating them,' Adam Jukes wrote in his book, *Why Men Hate Women*.

'Misogyny is as natural to men as the possession of a penis – its development is inevitable, and men are no more capable of fighting it as children than they are capable of being little girls.'[1] It was difficult to equate such words with the relaxed conversation that I was overhearing.

Statements about the universality of male misogyny raise men's hackles while stirring shouts of 'Right On!' from certain women, but the approach is too polemical and one-sided to provide a useful account of the complex feelings that men experience towards their mothers and then towards other lovers. There is no doubt that boys can hate their mothers with murderous intent: some psychoanalysts argue that every infant (boy or girl) wants to bite, tear and devour the breast of the 'bad' mother who looms over him. And nobody who has ever stood in a supermarket or on a railway platform and watched a mother trying to bring her boy under control could ever doubt a son's potential to feel rage against the woman who constrains and controls him. In this way he expresses his fears and his sense of impotence in the face of a woman whom he suspects is intent on damaging him, perhaps destroying him.

Yet the task of mothering (and fathering) is to give the boy a way to deal with these feelings so that he can bring them under control. It is only if his parenting is malicious or seriously inadequate that the hate of the 'bad' mother will not be balanced by at least some affection for the 'good'. The boy can out-grow such intense negative emotion by coming to recognise that this formidable figure will give up her power to him when he is capable of claiming it, and that those actions which he once interpreted as being against him were actually motivated by love for him, a desire that he should achieve his independence and prove himself.

Is this victory for love just a cover for all the hate that carries on simmering beneath the surface? Do men simply hide their anger against women because they fear the destructive impact of its release, sensing that it might even destroy them? Some argue that men's negative feelings never go away. Their anger, when it bubbles up, is all the more wild, violent and baleful in consequence of the efforts that have been made to repress it. But this is to claim that a cancer which has been in remission for two decades is still wreaking havoc in the body where it once had a foothold. Hate is always in competition with powerful drives to win love and make reparation for any damage that was once done. Often it will lose the battle, but it can also be controlled, and even the most destructive woman-hater is hungry for a woman's love.

The persistence of love in the midst of hate might seem to be a matter of no real significance. It is easy, after all, to mock the man who talks of his affection for the wife whose ribs he has just broken, forcing her into the sanctuary of a battered women's refuge. Many writers have done just that. But it induces a quite unnecessary pessimism to ignore the degree to which every heterosexual man longs to feel secure in a woman's arms and to enjoy the experience of a contentment and inner peace that he imagines to be possible there. It is absurd to claim that all men inevitably hate their mothers or their wives or women as a group, as if these feelings occluded all other emotion all the time. 'Male violence towards women,' says Susie Orbach, 'often conceals great feelings of vulnerability, feelings that cause such discomfort that they get transposed into fury.'[2]

Derek, a financier in his mid-forties, gives a series of reasons for the rage he freely admits to feeling against his mother. He remembers how she would humiliate him by playing jokily with his penis as she stood him up in the kitchen sink for a wash, so that any passer-by could see him through the window. He remembers her hitting him around the face with a slipper as he came in late at night. But most of all he remembers the problems that his mother had in showing him affection. 'Come and sit on your mother's knee for five minutes of love,' she would say, but ten seconds later she would push him away. When Derek asked why she was so sparing with her kisses and her cuddles, she would brush him off, replying that one day he would understand. Abandoned by his father when he was four, Derek felt that he had lost his mother to 'uncles' and to drink. She was either out of the house or down at the pub, or entertaining her men friends and taking no notice of her youngest son. He disliked the way in which she would dress up for other men, telling her that she should 'cover it up'.

The emotional aloofness of Derek's mother made him feel unloved; her lovers roused him to jealousy; her sensuousness and intrusiveness provoked feelings that he had no way of understanding. He entered adult life a true Lovelorn, hungry for the affection that he had never before experienced, always seeking out women who were dark-haired and brown-eyed as his mother was, then trying to win acceptance from them. 'I have had,' he says, 'lots of relationships with girls. I was looking for what I thought was love. I thought another person could make me feel good about myself.' But they never could.

None of my other interviewees found it quite so hard to speak of their experiences as Derek did. He chose to talk with me in a darkened room, with just one candle lighting up his scraggy frame and a large space interposed between us. He uttered jagged half-sentences, pushing out just a few words at a time, expressing the feelings of anxiety, insecurity and rage that had been thrown up in him by his experiences of getting close to women. At first he felt only an occasional surge of anger towards whoever had spent the night with him. 'I wanted to hurt her and beat her up,' he recalls. Gradually, though, he found his way to the source of those feelings. He was in his mid-twenties and his marriage was not going well. 'What,' he kept on asking himself while he was on top of his wife, 'would it be like to fuck my mother?' He would beat himself up about these thoughts, tell himself that it was not right to feel this way, but the idea of making love to his mother would then come back to him with still greater force. And there was nothing tender about the way he felt. 'It had to be hard, it had to be strong. Not loving intimacy, but crunch, crunch, crunch.'

Yet Derek always wanted to heal the ache that his mother stirred up in him, so that the love could win through. As a small child, he would seek to impress her by being smartly dressed for school, and ensuring that his shoes were better polished than those of his two brothers. 'If you looked immaculate,' he recalls, 'my mother thought everything was okay. I was always trying to please her.' He did what he could to soak up his mother's moods by adapting to them, blocking his own feelings and desires in the process. 'I became a chameleon,' he says. 'I had to fit in with whatever was going on. If she was happy, then I would be happy.'

Some thirty years on, Derek still wants to make things right for his mother by providing her with material comfort, and he has several times tried to establish a deeper connection to her. One night he shared a bottle of brandy with her in the hope that he could persuade her to talk about the past. Under the influence of alcohol she opened up a bit, but the next morning's sobriety drove her back toward the old patterns. 'I cannot get her to talk to me,' Derek complains. 'When we meet, we cuddle each other, say "It's lovely to see you," but it doesn't feel very real.' In parallel with this, Derek has sought healing through therapy, and in various men's groups, hoping that one day he will establish a strong, loving, mutual relationship with a woman, one which will enable him to feel at peace with himself.

What keeps on happening to Derek, as to other men who experience feelings of violent anger towards their partners, is that the pleasure found in intimacy and sexual ecstasy reminds him of their infantile complement, the experience of feeling himself to be helplessly in the charge of a woman who seemed cruel, callous and uncaring. Instead of feeling calm and satisfied by the experience, as other men might, he becomes unnerved, confused and bewildered. Instead of the gentle release anticipated, he finds himself in an experience that is bewildering and unnerving. And whereas, when he was an infant boy, he could find no way to express these feelings other than to bawl or retreat into depression, he now has available an adult's strength. He loses control and lashes out at the woman who has made him feel so uncomfortable.

Buster prided himself on a physical endowment and an understanding of female pleasure that enabled him to attract women who were bright, beautiful and willing to overlook his pot belly, his bulbous nose and his pock-marked skin. He found too that his position at the hard, selling end of a creative business made him interesting to women who liked to challenge his commercial outlook. One woman in particular provoked him so much that he decided he wanted to marry her. She seemed ideal. Her arguments reassured him that she was interested in him, bringing them together while also keeping them slightly at a distance. As long as they continued to dispute in cinemas, restaurants and nightclubs around town, he felt safe.

His prospective fiancée suggested that they should go on holiday together to see how they would get on when apart from friends and the city lights. Sitting over dinner one night in a Kenyan hotel, she tried to steer the conversation toward some topic other than the business in which they were both involved. His answer, revealing that he was not really interested in anything else, was like a light going out for her. Suddenly the quarrelsomeness that had excited her seemed simply boring. He could be the greatest lover in the world, but his lack of 'hinterland' made him of no further interest. She started to seek out the company of other, more interesting, people who were staying in the same place.

Buster recognised what was happening at once: it had happened before. Feeling that he did not matter any more, that he had no remaining control over this woman, he suddenly went for her one night, smashing her face and knocking her head against the wall. Later, while she washed the blood off her face, he wept. For weeks after they had returned home, he would send her flowers and offer her presents, which she refused. 'A baboon hit me,' she had told her friends when she returned to work. His love remained, his violence had been momentary, and yet the effect had been to destroy a relationship.

A man who does something so brutal and then denies it or says he was not himself at the time, blithely insisting that he wants to forget the matter and return to the situation as it was before, might seem to be guilty of the ultimate dishonesty. But he utters what is the simple truth for him. He cannot own these feelings, whose source lies deep in some primitive part of himself to which his mental processes have no access, because he has never begun to understand them. His partner may seem to know more about what sets him off than he does, which makes it all too easy to suggest that she must be to blame. He has to block out what he does not understand.

When Charlie found a new girlfriend after the wife whom he battered had thrown him out, he told her that he was not going to take any more 'shit' from women. 'And I don't,' he tells me firmly. Charlie has no inkling of how much happier he would be if he were to understand a little of his pain. His mother gave him no space in which he could explore his feelings, come to understand them and learn to deal with them. She was a formidable figure who largely ignored him, except when she thought that he needed a wallop or a clip around the ear, and his father was just a shadowy presence quite incapable of filling the gap. It was never possible for Charlie to talk to his mother about the things that concerned him, and he certainly cannot do it now. Although he goes to visit her once a week, and says that he is 'close', there is no intimacy between them. 'I have never,' he says, 'sat down and talked to her about my problems.'

Even when his wife expelled him from the house they

shared, Charlie's mother did not seem interested in what he was going to do with himself: it was as if she had written him off a long time ago, and her only concern was to ensure that her grand-daughters did not suffer too much distress. 'The rest,' says Charlie, 'was my problem and not hers.' And he has never found anyone else to whom he could reveal what was going on inside. 'To be honest,' he says, 'I don't really talk to anyone about emotional things. I seem to keep them all bottled up.' And he does not see the link between this repression and his violence, the fact that his response to every emotional problem is to lash out. When his wife told him to leave, it maddened him. Needing to do something decisive in the hope of staunching his pain, he ripped up the suits of his rival and threw them in the bin, then went after their owner with a billiard cue. The police were called and he was thrown into a cell to cool down.

It is because men are frightened of the sort of feelings that intimacy can throw up that they often become obsessed with exercising control in their relationships. Partly this is in the hope that, by restraining their partners, they can prove to themselves that they are not as powerless as they fear; partly too it is to try and enforce a form of contact that does not touch their sensitive areas. It is a man's fear, insecurity and lack of confidence in himself that lead him to exert a tight hold on the marital reins and, if the power balance shifts because his wife finds some way to establish her independence, he may crumble away to a shadow of his former, apparently self-sufficient, self.

The extent of a man's anger and violence against women is not determined by the degree of maltreatment or neglect he endured, but rather by the extent to which he was enabled to absorb and deal with whatever he experienced. It is the whole situation that determines his response. If he has a brother, father or uncle with whom he can share his pain, he will often be able to neutralise the effect of a callous mother upon his psyche. By cultivating other skills, he can gain a sense of his own capacity which enables him to say Boo! to his mother's desire for continued control over him. By later forming a relationship with a woman who enables him to understand that the person who loves him is no threat, he can master feelings of panic, despair and powerlessness.

Robert, a film-maker in his mid-thirties, was given many reasons to feel angry at the mother who bullied, embarrassed and humiliated him. He recalls his sense of disgust when he sat on a bus and watched diarrhoea running down her legs into high leather boots, then the horror of being forced to clean them. He remembers that, when he was nine, his mother used to parade in front of him wearing a see-through night-gown, which was behaviour that even at the time he considered to be 'gross' and 'inappropriate'. He remembers her screaming at him in a shopping mall. And he remembers her forcing him to write a letter to his stepfather, saying that he did not love him, which was the opposite of how he really felt.

But the worst thing that Robert's mother did was to throw him on the mercy of a man-hating grandmother, who would demonstrate her power by telling him that he had to clean the fish pond instead of going surfing with his friends, then spray him with a water hose because his whistling annoyed her (as it was meant to). She would lock the house against him, then beat him because he had outsmarted her and secured entry. 'Don't hit me,' he said to her on one such occasion.

'What are you going to do about it?' she replied, pushing against him and digging her nails into his arm.

'I'm going to hit you back,' he riposted.

'If you do that,' she said, 'you will be in a boy's home so fast you won't know what's hit you.'

At the age of fourteen, Robert decided that he could endure this persecution no longer. When he told his mother that he wanted to go, she replied, without revealing any emotion, that he would have to choose between a foster home and his stepfather. As Robert packed his clothes and other gear for the trip to his stepfather's house, he became aware that his grandmother was emptying his drawers onto the front lawn. She then moved out his aquarium and began stuffing underwear into the water. Running to the rescue of his fish, Robert was fought off by his grandmother wielding a broomstick. Kids from the neighbourhood gathered round and started to laugh. His mother looked on and did nothing. 'It is against nature,' Robert says. 'A mother should protect her young.' He did not see her again for six years.

When asked whether he can remember his mother ever showing him any affection, Robert draws a blank. He does, though, recall his own attempts to win some warmth from her by buying flowers and bottles of perfume with his weekly allowance. The results were disappointing. 'She didn't,' he says, 'know how to love.' The experience of neglect and abuse has left Robert prey to gloomy emotions. Thinking about his mother, he says, can put him in a really 'dark space', evoking feelings of insecurity and rage. It is because of her, he feels, that he is so afraid of 'not mattering, not being seen, not being loved'.

Yet Robert always felt able to fight back. Ultimately too he could assert himself by moving away, getting his own back on his mother and his grandmother simply by depriving them of any further opportunities to oppress him. A talkative, intelligent man who likes to play the clown, he learned to explore his feelings, to recognise them for what they were and to look for ways of bringing them under control. Thus, although his girlfriends can drive him into paroxysms of rage, he understands these emotions as responses to feelings of insecurity triggered in him by the relationship, which have their roots in his early experiences of his mother and grandmother, and he says that he has never lashed out physically against any woman.

Robert admits that his first experiences of women were 'scary', and that he found their sexual forwardness hard to deal with. When women wanted to sleep with him, it was difficult for him to feel relaxed and accept their overtures. 'I was afraid of getting close,' he says, 'then having them leave.' It was not until he found someone almost totally lacking in inner resources, who became completely dependent upon him, that he felt safe enough to enter into some sort of relationship. He describes the woman he eventually married as 'virginal', and says that he felt warmed by the way she clung to him, wanting to be always with him. Robert, for his part, felt confident that she would never leave him, and that she could never be attracted to another man.

But then, in the sort of see-saw swing typical of an Idolater, Robert began to chafe against the limitations of his relationship, feeling that he needed more out of marriage than he was getting. When he told his wife that he wanted to leave, she became hysterical, screamed at him and started to hurl flower pots over the balcony of their flat. He fled to his brother's house, took an undemanding job delivering groceries to old people and went off in search of casual sex. 'It didn't work,' he recalls. 'I couldn't get intimate, and not get intimate.' Within a short time, one of the 'casual' relationships had turned serious.

This new lover was no virgin, but a single mother with considerable sexual experience who had just come out of a relationship with a married man. These facts triggered all Robert's insecurities and stirred up feelings of jealousy more intense than any he had ever known before. The sex was 'amazing', but he could not cope with knowing that she had done something similar in bed a thousand times before. On every occasion when they made love, he would imagine her being in the same situation with other men. Terrified and fearful, Robert would get out of bed and punch the walls until his hands started to bleed.

For several years, Robert felt torn between trust and hate. For a while he would be buoyed up by his girlfriend's love and then, like an inflatable doll into which someone had plunged a pin, he would collapse. The anger and violence he felt would terrify him so much that he felt compelled to move out, then try to get back together with his girlfriend. He would have another go at forming casual relationships which did not evoke the same sort of intense feelings, but that did not work. At the time of his interview for this book, Robert and his girlfriend were back together again, but he talked about 'holding back', trying to keep a 'protective shell' around himself, attempting not to have feelings so strong that the violence would swell up in him all over again.

There are those who argue that all male violence against women is part of a conspiracy to maintain male power. 'As long as some men use physical force to subjugate females,' Marilyn French unhelpfully remarks, '*all* men need not.'[3] This is a style of generalising about men that ignores the emotional history behind such behaviour. What Robert describes is how the quest to find a loving, mutually satisfying relationship stirred up in him all the anger he had once felt against the women who sought to control him. That he did not become a batterer is probably due to his having been given an opportunity to escape from his persecutors. It could, though, have been otherwise. He might have found himself locked in some nightmarish psychological trap contrived by his mother and grandmother which made it seem quite impossible for him to leave. 'Checkmate!', he would have heard them say. His confidence destroyed and his anger stoked by the emotional batterings he had received, he might have felt that he had no choice but to smash down the guardians of his prison, the women who had deprived him of his power, his mastery, his masculinity. He might have done what Owen did.

In the village where he lived with his parents and his younger sister, Owen was generally considered to be a nice boy, although people recognised that he was a little quiet and broody. Although he had spent a year away from home, studying at the agricultural college nearby, his mother was quite determined that when he came back, he would stay to work the fields that his father rented from a local landowner. A chapel-goer and a forceful personality, someone very different from her meek husband, Owen's mother was generally considered to be vicious. With all the authority that she needed to enforce her will, she took her son to pray in chapel on Sundays and stopped him from watching soaps on television for fear that they would corrupt him. She paid him a pittance for the work that he did on the farm and, even when he was eighteen, she put the money directly into a bank account to which he had no access.

One Saturday, his mother made him stop in while his father went to the pub, and his younger sister attended a disco in another village. When he asked his mother why he could not have some money to go out, she told him to keep his trap shut. Why was his sister allowed to enjoy himself when he was not? he asked. That was different, she replied. Owen's mother had an answer to every question, and every answer seemed to tighten his chains, putting him into a greater rage. His despair was heightened by the fact that a friend whose parents treated him in a not dissimilar way had recently committed suicide. Feeling that he had been imprisoned by his mother, Owen saw his life stretching before him as a long, dark tunnel from which there was no possibility of escape. He went into a shed, picked up an axe, came into the sitting room and brought it down upon her head.

Some 250 policemen were called in to hunt for Owen. They dredged the estuary nearby, blocked the surrounding roads, scoured the ports and knocked on doors to see if anyone had caught sight of him. It was about two weeks after the murder that Owen woke up a social worker who lived next door to the family home and asked whether the funeral had been held. As he drank her tea, he revealed that he had never been more than 300 yards from his front door. The judge gave Owen a short prison term, apparently agreeing with many of the villagers that he had been provoked beyond enduring.

To any outsider, it might seem that Owen's action was

totally demented. He was a grown man, who could have walked out of the door, found himself a job somewhere else and never seen his mother again. But he needed some recognition from his mother that would give him the courage to take this step. He required her to recognise that he truly was a man before he could behave like one. Her blank refusal to give him what he was so clearly asking for, her insistence on treating him as if he still was a child, made him mad like a child, with the only difference being that he was now strong enough to act upon the resulting murderous impulses.

While male violence is obviously a problem of hate, it also represents a man's failure in his struggle to love, to contain the dissatisfaction he feels about his childhood experience, put aside despair and try for something better. No intimate relationship more represents the triumph of hope over experience than one entered into by a man who, although still haunted by images of women who are out to diminish and disempower him, tries to find the good in the women to whom he attaches himself. Unfortunately, he is often so constrained by his experiences of the past that he hitches himself to someone with whom he is bound to repeat them, perhaps in a far more devastating form.

'I always loved Monika,' said Michael Telling at his trial for her murder. 'If only she had stopped going on at me, this would not have happened. Even after she died, I wanted her to be with me.' Telling killed his wife shortly after breakfast. She was standing between two settees in the drawing room, knocking back a Benedictine mixed with orange, her usual morning tipple. He walked through the door, raised his handgun and fired three bullets. 'I was very confused in my mind at the time,' he recalled. 'I had no clear idea why I shot her.'

Telling shot his wife because he wanted to stop the chatter in his head. As far as he was concerned, his action did not reflect any change in his feelings towards her, although when she was a corpse and could no longer nag him, it was much easier to be with her. He set up a camp bed in an upstairs room, laid her cadaver upon it and installed an air freshener to draw out the smells. He then carried on his life as normal, making trips into town to take out money from Monika's bank account, returning regularly to kiss and talk to her rotting remains. When the smell became too much, he moved her to the sauna that was half-built in the grounds that surrounded their spacious house. And when he finally buried her in a wood, he kept Monika's head in the boot of his car. As he saw it, their love was going to last for ever.

Michael had hoped that in marrying Monika, he would find the love of which there had been little in his life to date. His father had been an alcoholic who beat him. His mother entrusted the tiresome job of child-rearing to a succession of nannies. Taunted at school for his sickliness, Michael was easy prey for bullies, who once rolled him in nettles and turned him into a screaming, swollen sore. Michael's first wife could not endure his moods and threw him out. He tried to repair his damaged ego, and bolster his sense of security by starting a collection of guns and driving around on a Harley Davidson motorbike. Lacking real friends, he became a ham radio enthusiast, with the codename 'Snake 99'. He visited nightclubs, went to parties and met the good-time girl who became his second wife.

But no woman could have been less suitable for Michael Telling than Monika Zumsteg. He needed someone gentle, tolerant, loving and consistent, someone who would help him work through a tortured past and find his way to modest happiness. Instead, he fell for an exotic beauty, a woman whose brash glamour and energetic pursuit of pleasure were thin covers for her own confusions about what she wanted from her life. Wild and wayward before she married Michael, that was how Monika remained. At every turn she brought back to him the confusions and humiliations of his childhood.

Michael used to fantasise that he could change his wife by wresting her away from drugs and booze. Provoked by his pleas, she took lovers, taunted him for his sexual inadequacies and increased her drug-taking. When he became maudlin and gloomy, she begged him to leave. And as his personality further crumbled, she tried to have him placed in a psychiatric hospital. He felt haunted by the persecuting demons of his past – his father, his mother, his teachers – who had similarly rejected him, labelling him deficient and defective. He was increasingly confused by his wife's changing moods. 'There were 101 reasons,' he said in explanation of what he had done. 'I can't really explain. She kept pushing me. I just snapped in the end. She was horrible in many ways.'

Press reports of Michael Telling's trial in 1984 were widely criticised for implying that in some way his wife had brought her fate upon herself, that it was she rather than the perpetrator whose guilt was under examination. Looking to ascribe blame and responsibility in this way is seriously to misunderstand the nature of the situation that is created when two people persuade themselves that they should spend time together and try to make each other happy, even though it is clear to any observant outsider that they have a disastrous effect upon each other. Both are brought together by the same sort of emotional perversity, by childhood experiences which left them confused and unhappy, ultimately too immature to handle the explosive emotions released in a relationship with someone very like themselves. Both are victims of parenting that was cruel or neglectful.

Moralising exhortation will not help a man who has no power to rein in his rage and repeatedly tries to bash women into a shape that he finds more satisfying. In order to encourage his loving side, he needs to be offered some chance to go down into the deepest recesses of his psyche, and to begin there the painful and difficult task of discovering just what it was that made him feel so angry in the past when he lived with his mother, and why he seeks out women who will stir him up all over again.

In the next chapter, I look at a seventh category of men, those who deal with their anger against women by becoming Seducers.

CHAPTER SIXTEEN

Seducers

I met Angus at the London house of a mutual friend. Hearing about my book, he remarked without further prompting that it was his mother's fault he was still without a wife even though he had been dating women for over forty years: he said, though, that he was still looking. I asked if we could have a chat. Only if I were to trek up to Scotland and visit him on the farm where he lives, he replied. Four months later, I surprised him by ringing from Edinburgh to make an appointment.

I reached Angus's house down a bumpy road. A rusting ambulance was mysteriously parked to one side of the entrance gate. The lawn's grass lay where it had fallen and its mowing was the only sign that any attempt had been made to bring the garden under control: there were bushes of untamed honeysuckle and a wilderness of purple and green behind the house. I told Angus that I loved the wild disarray of his garden. He replied sharply that it was not at all to his taste, and that his mother, who had died some twenty years before, would have been 'deeply horrified' to see it looking that way. Clearly, Angus's mother had disapproved of mess.

Although Angus protested that he was, by nature, a tidy person, the inside of his house gave further lie to his remarks.

To the right of the front door two portable television sets were piled on top of each other, with an old table-top model sitting alongside. A photocopier rested on the piano. By the battered sofa stood boxes overflowing with magazines and newspapers. The dining room table was strewn with toast crumbs, stray pieces of cutlery, a Weetabix packet and a pot of marmalade that had dried up inside. On the kitchen table were accumulated piles of sheets and boxer shorts, a clothes press, newspapers and invitations to various social events.

As we sat outside in the August sun, eating a bachelor's lunch of paté, smoked salmon and cheese, I asked Angus to elaborate on that remark about how his mother was responsible for his being still unmarried. His reply brought the conversation back to the subject of mess. She had, he said, been 'more critical than she should have been' of the girls he brought to stay in the large house that his parents owned. Their 'slummy habits' suggested to his mother that they would not 'run my set-up in the way that it ought to be run'. Some of them further alienated her by smoking, which she considered an unattractive vice.

So Angus's mother had made some sharp remarks about girlfriends some four decades earlier. This did not sound very convincing as an explanation of why a man of 61 should be without a wife. It seemed, though, that these maternal comments had touched off a conflict that smouldered deep within him: between his desire to respect her attitudes, and an equally strong determination to repudiate them. And it is that conflict which Angus still plays out in his attitudes to women and to relationships.

In the house where Angus grew up, things had to be just so. 'Everything,' Angus says, 'went like clockwork.' As a child who wanted his mother's love, which was not easily secured, Angus did not feel able to argue with her and assert his view that there was another, more relaxed and informal way to live. One part of him absorbed his mother's precepts and made them his own, to such an extent that when he visited the London flat of a girl of whom his mother did approve, and found that it was 'knee-deep in litter', he decided that it was best to reject her.

This obsessively-tidy voice is still strong in Angus. It is why he wants to convince me that he is naturally house-proud, when all the evidence points in the other direction. He offers numerous excuses for the way things are, blaming his nephew for the untidy piles of newspapers, the season for all the work that had not been done. 'I am unable to do much to improve things,' he says. 'It's laziness and a delight in being side-tracked.' But the untidy state of Angus's house and garden is also a protest against his mother's precepts. He is not just powerless to produce the order that he says he truly desires, but unwilling to do what he still views as his mother's bidding. And because that conflict was never fought to any sort of resolution with his mother, it is provoked by every woman that he meets.

Angus is enmeshed in a deep emotional trap. He is unable to accept the sort of homemaker that his mother prescribed for him, but he also cannot free himself sufficiently from her precepts to seriously look for someone else. It is as if he is continuously fending off the fear that he would be controlled by his wife as he had been by his mother: whatever contrary evidence is presented, he cannot believe in the possibility of a relationship where he would *not* be so controlled.

Angus preserves his bachelorhood by holding up two models of what he wants and refusing to prefer one over the other. One version is the sort who might win his mother's approval. The dozen women he has considered as serious marriage candidates all qualified themselves by being 'capable housewives' who could 'cope with the cooking and that sort of thing'. They were not 'career girls', were 'basically good-looking without being wildly beautiful' and they were 'not messy, either in their person or where they lived'. At the same time, Angus has been on the lookout for girls who were fast enough and wild enough to 'race his motor' and who would have shocked his mother, women in their early thirties or younger who had a 'bit of mileage left'. They also had to be slim 'single-bed' girls, who showed no sign that they would 'blow up' by putting on weight when they reached the menopause, as his mother had.

It may be because Angus's criteria for selecting a wife provide such an unpromising basis for marriage that he holds on to them so hard. At bottom, he is terrified of being ensnared by any woman. This is evident also from the tactics which he has adopted to ensure that all his relationships stay at a superficial level. Whenever he and his girlfriends go out together, he will continuously flirt with other females, in a way that is guaranteed to arouse jealousy in whoever happens to be his partner for the night. 'The drive back from parties with my own lady,' he says, sounding like a naughty boy caught in some misdemeanour that he considers minor, but of which others take a different view, 'has sometimes been a terrifying post-mortem of my behaviour.'

This determination to go on 'playing the field' and thus undermine real intimacy is strategic. Seeing women either as domestic tyrants who will knock his house and himself into unwelcome shape, or as objects of sexual attraction whose vital statistics will eventually and inevitably expand into unalluring grossness, he is unable to envisage any sort of relationship that would be endurable in the long term. Given that he holds such attitudes, he may be right to worry about the prospect that any marriage into which he entered would fail, bringing down upon him 'untold problems and untold expense'.

To call Angus a Seducer might be to glamorise his confused condition, and yet that is essentially what he is. He has a pressing need to be surrounded by pretty girls, to have the eyes of women upon him, and to enjoy intercourse with their bodies. He is hungry for pleasure, and yet he seduces only so that he may discard and then move on. He is unable to do anything with a woman he has sexually aroused other than to abandon her. Many boys treat girls like this in adolescence, but most go on to look for some sort of relationship that is richer, more ultimately satisfying. The Seducer never takes this step.

Just as adolescent promiscuity is a declaration of freedom from mother, so the behaviour of a Don Juan is a continuous protest against the power that mother had over him, and the demands that she made upon him. He tries to construct a relationship in which he can secure the most basic thing that he wants, access to her body, and yet she can ask nothing of him other than that he give her pleasure too. He may well prefer the company of prostitutes, because they will not make even that minimal demand. The Seducer sometimes seems to be after revenge, seeking to make women suffer by denying them just what it is that they want: love and true affection. He talks about his love for women, but his actions express resentment and dislike.

It is often implied that this Don Juan lurks in every man. That while women quest for intimacy, all men would prefer to notch up women as if they were numbers in a bingo game, the numerical score being more important than anything else. They settle into marriage, it is argued, only as a cowardly retreat before women's power and under strong social pressure. If they felt able to press a woman's buttons quite as efficiently as Don Juan, then perhaps they too would go a-roaming. Such an attitude ignores the power of a Seducer's fear and the enduring nature of his hate.

Even some thirty years after he left his mother's home in Christchurch, New Zealand, and fled to the other side of the world, Steve's feelings towards his mother are dominated by intense irritation. She was not callous, cruel or irresponsible, but she remained ever the boss. Her moods determined the emotional atmosphere of the house. She always wanted to know what her son was up to. When she did not get her way, she nagged and moaned until he gave in. And Steve's father, a 'mouse of a man', never complained about this sort of treatment and never took her on. He simply allowed himself to be bossed around. 'All the initiative and drive came from my mother,' Steve recalls.

Steve looked at the relationship between his parents, and at the pressure he felt coming off his mother, then came to the conclusion that this was not something that he could bear to endure himself. 'I did not,' he recalls, 'want to live like my father was living. I wanted to get out into the world and do things. I could see that women would be a millstone. I did not need to have a woman at my side. If anything, a woman is a bit of a nuisance.' Steve's attitude reveals an enormous lack of confidence in himself. He came to feel that he would inevitably be humiliated by any woman, as his father was. He could not believe in the possibility of establishing a relationship of rough equality, because he had never witnessed anything like it. He recognises his weakness, his inability to take on the challenge, by refusing to let a woman come close.

But he cannot simply leave it at that. Just as he wanted to prevail against his mother when he was a child, so he longs to get the better of women in later life. By entering relationships in which sex is separated off from intimacy, he feels that he can do just that. But even this is a dangerous step, against which he has armed himself by developing attitudes to women that are marked by deep contempt. 'I am not terribly impressed by women as a species,' he says. 'I think they are very much second division. They are shadows of men. They make a lot of noise, but there is not a lot of action.'

Steve wants sex, but he does not want a relationship. 'If I had somebody,' he says, 'who came around every Tuesday afternoon and we had two hours in bed with sex, that would be fine. Just a nice chat, a cup of coffee and out of the door. I don't want to really know the person.' There are, though, several obstacles to achieving this Nirvana. The 'great sex' often does not come until he has been with a woman three or four times, because he is usually nervous. And he tends to see women for six months or so, because he does not like the anxiety involved in going out to pick up new lovers. Inevitably, then, he starts to learn a little about the women he sleeps with, and they get to know him too.

All that Steve wants is the plunge into sexual ecstasy. He would like his relationships to be frozen at one particular point in their development, never to change. He thinks it absurd that he cannot have this perfect state because sex in his experience changes women's feelings about the relationship, so that they start expecting to be taken into account when he makes his plans. That is why, although he enjoys sex, he sometimes wishes he never had to go to bed with a woman. 'I like being in control,' he says, 'and I am in control before I go to bed with her. After that, I lose the upper hand. I am no longer free to come and go.' And six months later, when he is still stubbornly a Seducer, unable to change, she calls him the worst person in the world, throws his keys down the gutter and causes scenes in public. 'I think women are trouble fundamentally,' he concludes. 'They can all be a pain in the neck. It is always going to end in tears.'

Sex is so important to the Seducer because the deeper pleasures of relating are closed to him. Sex is not just part of the language in which he communicates with women, it provides the vocabulary and the grammar. It enables him to feel that he is close without becoming intimate, to sense that he has won the battle against women without ever needing to engage fully in conflict. He can relive the pleasure of blissful contact with a woman's body, without re-evoking the anger and frustration that his mother also made him feel. But although Steve is a Seducer, he is no Don Juan. His mother never taught him that there was a way in which he could win her over, by being nice to her. He has never learned fully to turn on the charm. 'I'm still slightly grateful for whatever comes along,' he remarks a little forlornly. The true Don Juan is a little more optimistic about his capacity to make women feel good even as he runs away from them.

Richard, a musician in his late fifties, was, of the people, men and women, whom I interviewed for this book, the one who strove hardest to make me feel welcome. His sitting room seemed to have been laid out for the comfort of his guests, and Richard made a considerable effort to accommodate my tastes as he laid out a splendid lunch for me, which we ate among the pot plants on his balcony.

Richard says that he has always known that he was attractive, finding at school that he easily accumulated a wide circle of admirers, without ever self-consciously trying to gather them around him. What explains his appeal? He says that he still does not know. 'I have,' he says, 'a small repertoire of seduction techniques which I lay on strong in relation to people I think are promising.' But then, when victory seems close, he withdraws. It is a recurring pattern in his life – attracting people, striving to win their affection, then stamping on them – that now fills him with self-disgust. 'I have a terrible tendency,' he says, 'to move one step forward and two back in relation to people all the time, and to sort of hold off in a very demanding and selfish way.'

Richard has had long-term relationships – was once even married – but he has never made a commitment to anyone, man or woman, that he planned to keep. He will live only with a woman who lets him roam as free as he likes, having affairs with whoever he likes, whatever sex they may be. The goal of his life, he tells me, is never to have to do anything for anybody else. Whenever someone tries to force him into facing up to his responsibilities, he throws a rage and charges towards the nearest exit.

He seems, for example, to have spent more time running away from his wife than he ever did trying to get close. When the possibility that they might become engaged was first raised, he fled to the United States, and spent a year in a sexual relationship with the wife of the man who had offered him a home, his mother's former lover. It was when this situation became too complicated that he returned to England, and only when his girlfriend became pregnant that he married her. Shortly afterwards he discovered the easy pleasures available on the homosexual scene, which enabled him to find alternative sexual outlets while maintaining the pretence that he was a faithful husband.

When Richard says that he is 'more gay than straight', he seems to be expressing his preference for casual encounters with men over relationships with women that all too often lead to demands for intimacy and contact, procreation and child-care. He has never had any sort of relationship with a man, just sex. Everything that Richard says about sex, including his reference to using it as 'part of a healing process', makes me feel that he tries to make connections to others through sex, rather than using sex to deepen his connection to others. When he remarks on his fascination with incest and under-age sex, saying that he regrets not having been 'sophisticated' enough to have a sexual relationship with his daughters, his remarks do not seem to take any account of the possible effect such dodgy sexual encounters might have on the other parties involved, his own children.

The pleasure that Richard obtains from sex seems to have more to do with securing physical release than with expressing love for another person. I asked him, for example, to elaborate on what he meant by a remark about sexual fulfilment being 'much easier to achieve with someone of your own sex', and he seemed impatient with what he took to be my ignorance. 'The point is,' he said, 'that orgasm is extremely easy to achieve with other males who want the same thing.' I wondered whether his irritation expressed his desire to fend off a facile remark from me to the effect that sex could be about something more than easy orgasms.

As Richard's daughters entered their teenage years, he found it difficult to tolerate the strain of living with three women, all of whom demanded ever-increasing attention from him. His wife was frequently depressed: she once woke up in the middle of the night when they were staying with friends and started to play the piano very loudly, until she had woken up everyone in the house. His daughters were noisy and as demanding as teenage daughters with delinquent fathers tend to be. It was when he was about to trade their terraced town house for a farmhouse in the country that Richard decided he could tolerate marriage no longer. Leaving his wife to the charity of his mother and some neighbours, he took off with a succession of girlfriends and squandered the proceeds from the sale of the family house on high living.

Richard's many liaisons since have always been constructed in such a way as to ensure that he never finds himself again in a situation so tricky, perilous and demanding. After finishing lunch, we came downstairs to find a woman scuttling around the kitchen. She was so quiet and withdrawn, putting me in mind of the way those who have been physically abused sometimes behave, that I assumed her to be one of Richard's daughters, recuperating from some crisis in her relationships. It took me a while to realise that she was in fact the woman with whom he now shares his life. Bringing us coffee, she showed no sign of being curious about the interview that was taking place. I wondered what she would think about the unflattering remarks that Richard had made about her, but sadly suspected that she had heard much worse from his own lips.

Unlike Richard's former wife, Eleanor is a woman who makes no demands at all. She never threatens him, never tries to constrict him, never asks insistently for anything. She would like children, but she talks about her desire so quietly that Richard can ignore the request. The fact that she does not rouse in him much sexual excitement makes it easier for him to wander off in search of other adventures. He need never worry that she will not be home to care for him, whereas other, more vivacious and vital lovers could drive him crazy with jealousy. He knows that he is the centre of her life, and that she will stand by him whatever happens, even when – as once occurred – he was put under arrest for committing an act of public indecency. Eleanor does what he asks and tolerates whatever rebukes or insults he chooses to toss in her direction. Richard describes her as a 'strange' and 'quiet' person who does not have many resources, and who makes him feel 'absolutely safe'. She accepts him as he is. 'It cannot be easy for her,' Richard says. 'On the other hand, it isn't easy for me, because I find it quite boring a lot of the time.'

Why is Richard so irresponsible? Why can he not accept a relationship which would entail another person being able to make demands upon him too? The roots of his behaviour seem to lie in the double rejection that he endured in childhood. Firstly, his father left the family home when he was only three months old, and had almost nothing to do with Richard as he was growing up. He was given very little help to process his questions about why this might have happened. His mother told him simply that his father's leaving was a truly despicable act, and when this serial monogamist turned up two wives on to ask whether his first would take him back, he had the door slammed in his face. Who was most guilty for the break-up? What had been his mother's role? Did his own arrival have something to do with it? Richard had no way of knowing.

Then, when he was less than five years old, his mother sent him to boarding school. The institution was a relatively enlightened one, but Richard has memories of screaming and yelling in misery on each occasion that he found himself abandoned on the steps. And while he can also see that there were good reasons for sending him away during the war, he feels that in reality his mother was just after having a good time for herself. 'I do sort of wonder,' he says, 'if it didn't enable her to screw lots of American servicemen.'

Needing to extract from his mother an indication that she loved him, and would do so however he behaved, Richard set out to win a commitment from her that was also a way of exacting his revenge upon her. He did this by having himself expelled from school for reasons that he either cannot remember or will not admit, but which probably involved theft and sex. He then went back to live with his mother. That year at home set the pattern, he feels, for the rest of his life. He became, he says, 'one of those tiresome people who was in and out of my mother's house, never quite standing on my own feet. What I was effectively doing was making tremendous demands on her and forcing her to feel bad.'

On one occasion, Richard asked his mother to offer up to him what she would so lavishly provide for her lovers. He was feeling miserable because his elder brother's girlfriend had just smashed his model aeroplane, and he went to ask her if, in compensation, he could make love to her. She refused and, although he never asked again, Richard clearly regrets that nothing happened. 'I have no notion,' he says, 'of whether she would have fancied it or not.'

While Richard may not have asked again for sexual favours, there were many other demands that he did make. He repeatedly asked his mother to bail him out financially, right up until the day she died. He would tell her to sell some family heirloom so that he could pay his garage bills, and when she said that she was fed up with supporting him, he would say that it would be the last time since he was about to land himself a job. If she still resisted, he would apply pressure until she gave in. This pattern is one that Richard has not broken even now: sponging off others so that he has never had to work seriously at his career, or commit himself to anything.

Even as Richard describes to me the many occasions on which he feels that he has been a moral coward, he wears on his face the smile of a man who knows that he can charm his way out of almost any situation. Because he recognises that he is desirable, he does not feel the need to take account of anybody else's desires. His power to draw others to him is something that he needs to be continuously testing and re-affirming, because it is the only support that he has for his self-esteem; simply because he relies upon nothing else, he has been a failure as a husband, a parent and a friend. The ultimate impression when you speak to such a man is of his sadness.

The Seducer is inevitably dissatisfied by life because his true goal, to conquer his fear of mother and establish a relationship of intimacy with her, is one that he does not ultimately have the courage to undertake. Don Juan is not to be envied, he is to be pitied.

Conclusion

'I'm fifty years old,' says Sheldon Mills, the character played by Woody Allen in his short film *Oedipus Wrecks*,[1] 'I'm a partner in a big law firm, I'm very successful and yet I still haven't resolved my problem with my mother.' The film goes on to depict his archetypal Jewish Mama behaving in a way that no son could easily endure: she intrudes into formal office meetings, expresses disapproval of the woman he wants to marry and embarrasses him by recounting tales of his bed-wetting to anyone who will listen. 'I love her but I wish she would disappear,' Sheldon declares to his shrink, after which she obligingly vanishes for a while, only to re-appear as a heavenly wraith detailing her son's inadequacies to a chorus of sympathetic mothers gathered on the streets below.

During his Mama's all-too-brief absence, Sheldon experiences renewal: he feels relaxed and uninhibited for the first time in his adult life and there is a dramatic improvement in his sexual performance. But mother's celestial return causes the couple to squabble and the love to drain out of their relationship. It is only when Sheldon finds himself another woman, one who treats him like his mother, stuffing him with boiled chicken and fussing over him constantly, that the pestilential wraith stops her heavenly hounding and comes back to earth. The cycle of matriarchal power, the film suggests, can never be broken.

Some adult men are quite helpless to stop their mothers from phoning them, embarrassing them and generally bossing them around. Many more escape from mother only to find that they carry a residue of the tension, anger and distrust that mother provoked into their relationships to other women. In the film, when Sheldon's girlfriend Lisa suggests that the solution to his problem might be to move out of New York, he replies that it would do no good, since his mother would follow them. A man can flee to the other side of the world, but if his mother still occupies a large place in his head, he has no way to break her hold. His experience of her will shape his view of himself, how he looks at other women and what anxieties they arouse in him. Does he sometimes seem over-sensitive? Is he concerned to prevent any woman from securing the upper hand in an argument? Does he expect more freedom for himself than he allows to her? Or can he talk about what he feels, share his life experiences, openly discuss his plans and ideas. In all these areas, no man can easily escape from the pattern of his early life with mother.

She is so important an influence because the relationship he has with her is his first, and it gives her so much power over him. Having spent the first years of his life in hopeless thrall to her, needing her, pining for reassurance that he was loved by her, seeing the world through her eyes, while she guided him, pointed things out to him, helped him, encouraged him and bullied him, he cannot ever feel fully powerful in her presence, or spontaneously learn how to distinguish his own desires from hers. She defined his reality for so long that even the style of his rebellions is shaped by her.

It is not often nowadays that Jana feels much sympathy for her husband Milos, whose emotionally perverse behaviour she has long found quite intolerable. But his mother's reply when Jana told her over the phone that her son Jason was approaching some important exams shocked her into looking at Milos anew. 'He must get good grades,' the grandmother had said. 'My son has let me down and my grandson must not do the same. All my hopes are in him.' Was this, Jana asked herself, why her husband could never stop working so as to talk with his sons? Did his mother's continuous reminder that he had left Prague without taking a degree, without leaving a diploma for her to hang on the wall, mean that he was still struggling to come to terms with the sense that he was a failure? Could nothing he did ever make up for that fateful decision? Was it because he could not acknowledge this pain in his life that he could never talk about *any* of his feelings?

Every mother-son relationship contains the relics of its past, simmering beneath the friendly or not-so-friendly surface, waiting to be stirred up by a chance remark or deed. A mother's expressions of concern may take her son back to his helpless infancy and all its concomitant frustrations. By reminding her son of how dependent he once was, she can raise doubts about his capacity to hold on to adulthood. By clinging to the past that they shared, and expressing views that reflect her knowledge of his precarious development, she confronts her son with certain 'truths' about himself and how he came to be the way he is, that he may find difficult to hear. Whether it is her anxiety that demoralises him, her repressive power that constricts him, or her unhappiness that fills him with guilt, the emotions that she stirs up in him can overwhelm him.

It is because his mother's voice is powerful, resonating so deeply within him, that he will often feel so vexed by her. He may be angry with her for loving him too much and crushing his autonomy, or for not loving him enough and failing to feed his self-confidence. He may resent the way she preferred him over the other men in her life, or rage at her for never having protected him against his father's venomous temper, or for failing to provide him with any father at all. Even when he is married with three adult children of his own, he may feel her constantly at his shoulder, judging him, assessing him, rebuking him, smothering him, trying to control him, capable of rousing him to the heights of anger and distress.

Yet, because he still wants her love, he cannot simply give her up. However red-hot their relationship may be, he will not just walk away from it; because she knows too much about him, because she has such decided views upon his performance, because his habit of listening to what she says is too firmly entrenched, and because he loves her still. Even if he pulls out the phone and refuses to answer her letters, he will suspect that she is thinking about him, maybe talking about him; and he will recognise too the many ways in which she shapes him still. Not all the time, perhaps, just on the occasions when intimacy with others reminds him of how he once longed for her and feared her.

The relationship that a boy has with his mother is so crucial that it is all too easy for a man to blame her for everything that happens to him. If he is dissatisfied with his career, he may tell her that she is responsible for the misdirection of his life. If he cannot establish a satisfactory relationship with a partner, that too may be laid at her door. And he would be right to suggest that if he does not know what he wants from his life or relationships, it is because the stifling emotional atmosphere of his childhood prevented him from discovering the nature of his desire. Not, of course, that mother was the only one responsible.

It is all too easy for a man's emotional life to become mired in images of his mother. Looking for an opportunity to experience again the pleasure he once enjoyed in mother's arms, or wishes that he had, he either marries a woman who reminds him of his mother, or treats the woman he marries as if she was his mother, forcing her to become more and more like her as she tries to fill the gaps that he creates by being timid, slothful or wild. 'It seems to me,' says psychotherapist Heather Formaini, 'that one of the greatest problems is that there are very few men who really marry women they love.

They marry a woman who fits the kind of categories that they feel they ought to marry. Within a very short time, they have turned her into their mother.'

Instead of growing and maturing in such a relationship, the man congeals, because he is always trying to avoid feeling the anger, fear and confusion that can be so easily re-evoked in him by this woman. While she touches his longing for love and affection, she also stirs tension and anger. He cannot see his partner as a real person, only as a version of his powerful, controlling, dangerous mother. He is still fighting with old ghosts and demons, so that he cannot be reached when the woman he lives with begs him to listen to her, get close to her, tell him what he feels. A friend once asked me how she could 'wash' the mother out of her man. She could see how he had been shaped by the relationship he had with his mother, recognised that this was the source of the problems in their relationship, but had no idea what she could do about it. Her lover was in his early sixties.

Time and worldly success sometimes enable a man eventually to look at his mother in a different light, to see her as she really was and to accept her. Michael, now a judge in his early fifties, recalls that he once would have had great difficulty in finding a good word to say about his mother. Having started life as the daughter of an alcoholic village blacksmith, she had raised herself into the ranks of the middle-classes by becoming a nurse and marrying a docor. The defensiveness she felt about her past seemed to prevent her being open with her children and showing them affection. 'She never kissed me and I never kissed her,' Michael recalls. 'She never put her arm around me or I mine around her.' For years he railed against the way she treated him. His anger expresed a fear that he might become much more like her than he would wish to be.

A few years before she died, though, Michael began to recognise just how impressive was his mother's journey from apprentice seamstress to lady's companion, nurse and doctor's wife. While still repudiating her class hang-ups, he was no longered angered by them as he had been before. He recognised for the first time since early childhood that she had been good-looking and dressed elegantly. He saw how hard she had worked to keep his father's medical practice going. She was also, he now recognised, honest and scrupulous. And he could acknowledge too how much his own career success owed to the ambitions she had for him.

'I can only speak well of her now,' he says.

A man may also extricate himself from the maternal trap by finding a partner who triggers his affections without reminding him of his first love. Because he recognises her as someone separate, he can discover who she really is, without being overshadowed by the image of the great matriarch. What gives a relationship this transformative power is something of a mystery. It helps if the partners are young and not too much jaundiced by past failures, if they feel relaxed and open to new experiences, if they sense their lives are basically on track. Andrew gives a nightmarish account of life with his intrusive mother, who would follow him when he went out on dates with girls and used to march into the bathroom to have a good look at his genitals. 'She wanted to continue to control me,' he says, 'in the way that she had completely controlled me as a young boy.' He was actively involved in student politics and drama when he met the woman who has been his wife for twenty years, and she helped him to leave behind his anxieties about women. 'I guess I was lucky to find my wife,' he says. 'She is fairly easy-going. I think that if it had have been with someone else, it might not have been the same at all. I learned a lot from her.'

It is no solution, though, for a man to simply bump along from relationship to rocky relationship, hoping that one day he will get lucky and find a woman who will help him to grow up. What has to change is a man's attitude to women, and all too often the rituals of serial monogamy are deployed so that he can avoid facing up to what he does to undermine his relationships. Whenever he is touched to the raw so that he feels exposed and in danger, he moves on, never tackling what it is that disturbs him. He kids himself into thinking that the problems in his experience of women can be put right in subsequent relationships, but he will not do the emotional work that would be necessary if he were ever to understand his own blind spots, the source of all his problems.

Sometimes, when a relationship breaks down, the ensuing shock may lead a man to re-examine his attitudes to himself. Henry was mortified when his girlfriend, the woman with whom he had travelled the world for six months, whom he had thought would one day become his wife and bear his children, said that she was leaving him. He tried for a while to ignore her accusation that he never told her what he was feeling, remarking to his friends that he would have been happy to spew if she had ever asked him. 'I didn't think that she would be particularly interested,' he declared. But slowly he started to wonder whether she might not have been a little right. When he found himself another partner, he tried talking to her, and he says that the experience was 'truly liberating'.

There is also no doubt that Terry, whom I described in the chapter on Chauvinists, now repents the mistakes that he made in his marriage. 'I know that it is wrong what I did,' he says. He should, he feels, have been more relaxed about allowing his wife to do what she enjoyed, and should have worked harder to put some fun into the life they had together. He also has a lot more respect for what his wife used to do in the house now that, when he goes home, he has to cook the dinner for his son (who fled from his mother's care to be with dad), and a large part of each weekend is devoted to cleaning the house where they both live. 'I don't want to get into a relationship,' he says, 'just to go home for someone to be there. I would do my bit. I would come home and offer to do the washing-up or put out the washing.' Whether Terry would carry through on this resolution is, of course, an open question.

Psychotherapist Susie Orbach once suggested that the way for a woman to make a man more emotionally responsible was to withdraw her labour. One might call this the Lysistrata Solution after the Aristophanes comedy about a group of Athenian women who bring the Peloponnesian War to a halt by going on a sex strike. Superficially, the approach seems quite appealing, but it could also be counter-productive. When a man feels threatened and out of control, he is more likely to experience paranoia and lash out with violence than be motivated to examine himself. In this way, he struggles to cover over the very vulnerability that his partner seeks to expose.

The consequences of using the strike weapon are also extremely unpredictable. A few years before our interview, Gus's wife had become estranged from him, which led to her sleeping in the spare room for a few months. His experience of lying alone in the marital bed brought back to Gus his childish longing to have a 'wife' by his side. Reflecting upon his early experiences, he started to talk with a woman he knew from work, and to feel towards her emotions that he had never known before. He came to realise how much sex had always been for him about the relief of tension and the satisfaction of physical need, rather than an exchange of loving feelings. For the first time in his life, at the age of 42, he had discovered a desire for real intimacy. At the time of our interview, it was unclear whether this realisation would enrich his marriage, or end it. He did not know if he could find what he was looking for with a woman he had married for quite different reasons over a decade before, or would have to look for someone else.

It is clear that curing the ills of masculinity in adult men is a hard task; and it would be much better to prevent their development, so that boys could grow up with the ability to make the sort of connections to others that would lead to truly satisfying relationships. Since the problems of men seem to derive from exposure to too much mum and too little dad, the solution would seem to be simple: spread the responsibility for parenting evenly between mothers and fathers. 'My view,' argued Nancy Chodorow in *The Reproduction of Mothering*, 'is that single exclusive parenting is bad for mother and child alike.'[2]

This is not because any child can have too much of a mother's love, guidance and influence; nor because mothers are dangerous swamps from which boys must be extricated if they are to become men; nor because there is some part of the process by which a boy becomes a man that a mother is inherently incapable of helping him through, but because all children benefit from being exposed to two (or more) parental figures.

Whether the other parent is completely absent, generally delinquent or just not a very effective presence, a boy who grows up predominantly in the care of one parent is likely to be over-exposed to that carer's needs and power. Hating at times the control that this parent exerts over him, he needs opportunities to express his negative feelings so as to make space for the expression of the love he also feels. He will worry about the needs that the parent of whom he knows so much is not having satisfied elsewhere, and feel responsible for bringing some sort of relief. And if the primary parent is a woman, as is usually the case, the experience can generate in the boy the sort of dark, angry feelings towards the feminine that can never quite be thrown off. 'Under the arrangements that now prevail,' wrote Dorothy Dinnerstein some twenty years ago, 'a woman is the overwhelming external will in the face of which the child first learns the necessity for submission, the first being to whose wishes the child may be forced by punishment to subordinate its own, the first powerful and loved creature whom the child tries voluntarily to please.'[3]

If there is another such figure in his life, the boy's

observations of how his carers interact will help him to appreciate a richer variety of ways to relate than he can come up with on his own, and to be less rigid in the patterning of his relationships. His carers' togetherness removes from his shoulders the feeling that he must work to sustain the person upon whom his care depends. His awareness that there are two people of whose love he is reasonably certain gives him more freedom to experiment in how he will relate to them. He may irritate one and flee to the other, talk to dad when mum will not listen, bouncing off his parents like a dodgem car hitting against rubber-lined walls. And because he is not dependent upon only one parent for his life, his food, his sense of safety, he can feel confident enough to express more of what he wants or feels without being afraid that he is about to deprive himself of continued care.

For the men in this book, the weakness of their fathers tended to provoke denigration while their absence could inspire idealisation, and both positions left them confused about their own role in relation to the woman who was their mother. Their sense of being helplessly in thrall to a powerful feminine creature stirred up their terror of impotence and their fantasies of omnipotence. Trapped uncomfortably between these extremes, it was difficult for any sort of reasonably open relationship to emerge. Since they were not able to appreciate that their fathers were concurrently strong *and* weak, they found in them only a half-echo of their own feelings and anxieties. Because they received so one-sided a vision of father, whether as a man of steel or figure of straw, their answers to the question of what it meant to be a man necessarily lacked sophistication, tending to hinge on radical differences between men and women rather than the similarities between them.

Will the ills of masculinity really fall away if parents take equal responsibility for parenting, in order to ensure that boys and girls experience them both as fully rounded beings? Is the answer for fathers to spend more time pushing prams, changing nappies and ferrying their children around various social events; playing with them, talking to them, disciplining them, educating them? Was Nancy Chodorow right when she anticipated that 'equal parenting would leave people of both genders with the positive capacities each has, but without the destructive extremes these currently tend toward.'?[4]

The argument is that if mothers and fathers are equally free to parent and to work outside the home, every element in the domestic triangle will profoundly shift. Having enjoyed a more satisfactory experience of their own fathers, no longer burdened with any particular reason to envy men their freedom, mothers would approach the relationships with their sons in a more relaxed way. No mother would want to hold her son especially close, or punish him particularly severely, or express resentment against him, just because he was a boy.

The effect of such an arrangement upon the father would be even more marked. Participating equally with his partner in child-rearing, he would have an opportunity to make contact with all the vulnerability that men tend to run away from. 'What happens for the father when he is involved,' says psychotherapist Heather Formaini, who was researching a book about fathers when I interviewed her, 'is that he unlocks something inside himself and begins to relate to himself in a new way. I think you have an immensely creative situation where there is a threesome of two parents and a child.'

Under this arrangement, the boy would no longer experience his mother as such an over-bearing figure, both because her attitude to him would change, and because he would have a much stronger relationship with his father to set against it. His struggle to become an individual would not be defined so much in terms of gender, since his passage to maturity would involve breaking away from both a man and a woman at the same time. 'If the boy grows up with an active and engaged father,' suggests Susie Orbach, 'his identification with masculinity can occur in conditions of security rather than in an implicit repudiation of the feminine.'[5]

However strong the argument, though, implementing such a proposal is inherently problematic. How do you change men without changing the fathers who are men? If men are insensitive and irresponsible, there is little hope of persuading them to be good enough parents to ensure that their sons do not turn out the same way. The solution to the problem seems to require the solution to the problem. And how, also, do you persuade women to consider sharing parental responsibilities on an equal basis with men when, in their disgust at reports of male violence, sexual abuse and general unpleasantness, a growing number of them have decided that the influence of fathers upon their offspring is so potentially damaging that it is best disposed of? At a time when relations between men and women sometimes seem to be at a crisis point, with more and more women fleeing from marriage, deciding to have babies outside any relationship, or finding themselves landed reluctantly with a baby but no relationship, to argue that men and women should not only love each other more, but spend more time loving their children, could seem to be like preaching celibacy inside a brothel.

Also, men are not going to be persuaded to take on full parental responsibility, and women are not likely to give it to them, for as long as it seems that what is being discussed for fathers is just taking half of what women have been doing. The argument knocks too hard against inherent assumptions about gender difference. Just as the first thing that girls learn about their gender is that they will develop the capacity to be like mother, so boys learn that masculinity involves not being able to do what mother does. While that picture may soften over time, elements of it will probably remain. For the boy, the knowledge that a woman's body was his first home, and that he will never carry a baby as his mother did, sets him off on the quest for an answer to the question of what his maleness is all about. However much a boy experiences a warm and loving relationship with his father, he will never know the same sort of burning desire to become a parent that many women experience. 'For some,' remarks columnist Katharine Whitehorn, 'it is an incubating fever: it is a drive that builds with increasing insistence, like drums coming nearer. For such women, wanting a baby is as powerful and irrational an urge as sex itself.'[6]

A man may develop toothache as his partner's body swells, attend all the same pre-natal classes and (inappropriately) demand attention for his own needs in the labour ward, but ultimately he must deal with the fact that he will never carry a baby. This does not mean he cannot find his own reasons for longing to reproduce, nor that his emotions will not be profoundly stirred by an infant's arrival, but the limitations of his biological participation in the birth will necessarily influence his attitudes to parenting, and the role that fatherhood plays in his definition of himself.

'I used to feel,' remarks Yvonne, 'that I had been dealt nasty cards and that I would have done much better if I had been a man. Then I had a child. Only a woman can do that. It is something that makes you feel so whole. It reconciled me to being a woman.' Although Yvonne's husband has played an active role in parenting, the message which her son has picked up from her is not an egalitarian one. 'I think,' says Joe, 'my mother does a bit more than my dad, because she feels more responsible. That is because she made me. I didn't come out of him. My mother felt that she couldn't do anything when I was inside her, when I might have died or something. So when I came out, she wanted to make sure that nothing did happen to me. In a way it is reasonable. My father is as responsible as he can be.' Joe went on to describe in graphic terms the agonies that his mother had to endure as a result of his late arrival. 'She was getting very annoyed,' he said, 'going to horror films and drinking milk shakes.' He was not clear about the significance of the milk shakes.

Joe sees his mother as being more involved with him than

his father is, or could be. He might have felt differently if his father had participated even more than he did, insisting that his wife hand over a larger share of parenting responsibilities. But even if he had done that, it is likely that his mother's continued identification as his first home would have given her a distinct and gendered place in Joe's consciousness. And it would seem unlikely then that he could come to see nurturing as having given him as much of a role in life as a girl secures from the discovery that babies grow in women's bellies. Granted that gestating does not necessarily lead to responsibility for rearing, could the majority of boys really accept that parenting was their function just as girls do, given that milk does not flow from their breasts and babies do not grow inside their bodies? 'What cannot change,' says child psychiatrist Sebastian Kraemer, 'is that the child has never been inside the father, who in that sense must always represent something outside.'[7]

'It seems not to occur to most men,' says Marilyn French in a patronising tone, 'that they can, like women, find their centre in children.'[8] The mistake is to think that men can relate to their children in the same way as mothers do, or that the idea of fatherhood can provide a satisfactory initial answer to the question of what it means to be a male. Accepting this argument does not, though, mean that women should retreat to the home while men should get back to bread-winning; only that it is counter-productive to suggest that what is being discussed is the embrace by men of their 'feminine' side and the imminent victory of 'feminine values'.

Men might take up that sort of challenge, just as they once obeyed their mother's imperious commands, but their participation will be reluctant, angry, resentful. Psychotherapist Andrew Samuels has written about a 'new kind of man' who is a 'loving and attentive father to his children, a sensitive and committed marital partner' but an utterly miserable individual. His problem, as Samuels sees it, is that he is 'doing what he does to please Woman'.[9] Men who become participant fathers because they are ordered home to make up the baby's bottle and told that henceforth they are to be stripped of any freedom to wander, are likely to respond with more paranoia than love. Seeing before them terrifying images of mother with her fists raised, and her kitchen knife at the ready, they think about retreating into the woods where they can beat their drums in peace.

It is no solution, then, for fathers to embrace the parenting role in an attitude of defeat, because it is the only option left to them now that the factories have been demolished, the armed forces have been decimated, there are no jungles left to explore and women have anyway taken over. The good fathers are those who feel that they have something distinctive to contribute to the rearing of the next generation, who parent in their own way without deferring to women who claim to know the right way because their kind have been doing this for millions of years. And they need to somehow feel that, by embracing the challenge of forming a deep relationship with their children, and helping them to become full, rounded beings, they too can increase the richness of their lives, the range of their emotional repertoire, the breadth of satisfactions available to them.

Boys and men must learn that masculinity is not something that will forever be defined for them by school-teachers, toy manufacturers, Hollywood film-makers, childcare gurus, feminists and fathers, but rather a personal choice about how they want to live their lives that they freely make by listening to their own desires, within the experience of full relationships to parents, relations, friends and others. Masculinity, as I have said, is a question to which there are many different answers, and telling men that they must be fifty per cent parents can seem no less prescriptive than instructing them to be warriors or breadwinners.

Egalitarian parenting can, in the end, only be one part of the solution to a much wider problem, which is how you construct a situation in which the voices of boys (and girls) can find a hearing, so that, in talking about what they feel, children may explore what they want to be and have a real choice about what they will become. 'We find children's lives difficult to respond to,' writes Susie Orbach, 'because we are habituated to ignoring, suppressing, disregarding our own.'[10] At a time when children are being brought up in many different family situations, with parents who hate each other, parents who love each other so obsessively that they have no time for their children, and parents who have not exchanged a word for years, children need to be offered new ways to deal with the consequences of growing up in the wake of the problems that adults have in relating. How can the boy who confronts a mother's tyranny, a father's cruelty or the sense of being caught helplessly in the middle of a struggle between them, so that he feels powerless, unloved, utterly without value, be helped to salve the pain and resolve the difficulties that he faces every day of his life?

'We ought to assume,' Bruno Bettelheim wrote, 'that whatever a child does, however outlandish or foolish his behavior may seem on superficial observation, he has excellent reasons for engaging in it. If we start out with this assumption, we will search for its meaning, and the more incomprehensible the behavior the more seriously we then search.'[11] Such a form of listening becomes steadily harder to achieve. The pressures of modern life mean that many parents are too busy, too preoccupied, too troubled, too anxious, too much tied up with their own problems, to take sufficient notice of what their children are trying to say. Instead of being encouraged to express what they feel at the dinner table or in a one-to-one confessional, boys are allowed to lock up their feelings, smothering them in front of the TV, the computer screen or the glue bag, perhaps diverting them into acts of petty vandalism and compulsive sex. And when they sulk, throw a mood, commit an act of violence or turn to serious criminality in an attempt at drawing attention to the angst they feel, their communications are more likely to be met by silence, a reproach or punishment than by serious listening. They are left on their own to develop whatever desperate coping mechanisms they can squeeze out of their tortured psyches.

It does not seem likely that the family can be relied upon to create spaces in which today's children can explore their emotions. Boys and girls need to feel that there are other doors through which they can go in search of someone who will listen. They might benefit from programmes of group therapy within schools, in which they could be encouraged to articulate the problems they are having, and become used to the idea that it is okay to state that one is feeling lonely, sad or angry. If teachers were not so over-burdened, they could play an even greater role than they do in attending to the communications that children offer about their experiences. Whatever course is followed, the ills of masculinity can only be healed by giving all boys and girls the means to voice their feelings, so that they can come to understand exactly how their actions are shaped by their emotions.

Notes

Chapter One 'Mothers of Men'

1   *Observer*, 22 May, 1994
2   Adrienne Rich, *Of Women Born: Motherhood as Experience and Institution*, Virago, 1986, p. 193
3   Estela Welldon, *Mother, Madonna, Whore*, Free Association Books, 1988, p. 88

Chapter Two 'Power With Security'

1   Andrew Samuels, *The Political Psyche*, Routledge, 1993, p. 140
2   Luise Eichenbaum & Susie Orbach, *What Do Women Want?*, Michael Joseph, 1983, p. 61
3   Christiane Olivier, *Jocasta's Children*, Routledge, 1989, p. 42
4   Dinnerstein, *The Rocking of the Cradle and the Ruling of the World*, Women's Press, 1987, p. 66
5   Louis Althusser, *The Future Lasts a Long Time*, Chatto and Windus, 1993, p. 106

Chapter Four 'Crossing the River'

1   Carol Lee, *Talking Tough: The Fight for Masculinity*, Arrow, 1993, p. 44
2   Robert Stoller, *The Transsexual Experiment*, Hogarth, 1975, p. 35

3 Christiane Olivier, *Jocasta's Children*, p. 15
4 Angela Phillips, *The Trouble with Boys*, Pandora, 1993, p. 43.

Chapter Five 'Wild Men'

1 Alessandra Piontelli, *From Fetus to Child*, Routledge, 1992, p. 1
2 Piontelli, *op. cit.* p. 225–31

Chapter Six 'Inside the Triangle'

1 Elias Canetti, *The Torch in My Ear*, André Deutsch, 1989, p. 120
2 Canetti, *op. cit.*, p.120.
3 Freud, *The Interpretation of Dreams*, 1900, *SE* 4 & 5, p. 262
4 *Oedipus Tyrannus* (tr. Vellacott, *Sophocles and Oedipus*, Macmillan, 1971), lines 982–3
5 Robert Bly, *Iron John*, Element, 1990, p. 18
6 Ludovic Kennedy, *On the Way to the Club*, Collins, 1989, p. 58
7 Andrew Samuels, *The Political Psyche*, Routledge, 1993 p. 29
8 Bly, *op. cit.*, p. 16
9 Heather Formaini, *Men: The Darker Continent*, Mandarin, 1991

Chapter Seven 'Lover Sons'

1 *Collected Letters of D. H. Lawrence*, Viking, 1962, Vol. 1, p. 69–70, quoted in Kate Millett, *Sexual Politics*, Rupert Hart-Davis, 1971, p. 247
2 *The Letters of D. H. Lawrence*, Viking, 1932, p. 245, quoted in Millett, *op. cit.*, p. 78
3 D. H. Lawrence, *Sons and Lovers*, Cambridge Edition, 1992, p. 43

Chapter Eight 'Breaking Away'

1 Edna O'Brien, *Time and Tide*, Hamish Hamilton, 1993, p. 254
2 Bruno Bettelheim, *A Good Enough Parent*, Thames and Hudson, 1987, p. 161
3 Olivier, *op. cit.*, p. 40

Chapter Nine 'Chauvinists'

1 Claude Lévi-Strauss, *The Family*, 1956, p. 269, quoted in Nancy

Chodorow, *The Reproduction of Mothering*, University of California Press, 1978, p. 35

Chapter Ten 'Man's Desire'

1   Stoller, *op. cit.*, p. xvii
2   Oscar Hijuelos, *The Mambo Kings Play Songs of Love*, Farrar, Straus, Giroux, 1989
3   Dinnerstein, *op. cit.*, p. 60
4   Ludovic Kennedy, *op. cit.*, Collins, 1989, p. 71
5   Camille Paglia, *Sexual Personae: Art and Decadence from Nefertiti to Emily Dickinson*, Penguin, 1991, p. 20

Chapter Twelve 'Give me Love, Baby!'

1   Chodorow, *op. cit.*, p. 104
2   Elias Canetti, *The Tongue Set Free*, André Deutsch, 1977, p. 37
3   Bettelheim, *op. cit.*, p. 223

Chapter Thirteen 'Emotional Block'

1   Angela Phillips, *op. cit.*, p. 60
2   Bettelheim, *op. cit.*, p. 89

Chapter Fourteen 'Trad Men'

1   Bly, *op. cit.*, p. 2

Chapter Fifteen 'Lashing Out'

1   Adam Jukes, *Why Men Hate Women*, Free Association Books, 1993, p. 11
2   Orbach, *What's Really Going On Here*, Virago, 1994, p. 69
3   Marilyn French, *The War Against Women*, Hamish Hamilton, 1992, p. 184

Conclusion

1   *New York Stories* (1989), Tri-Star Pictures

2 Chodorow, *op. cit.*, p. 217
3 Dinnerstein, *op. cit.*, p. 28
4 Chodorow, *op. cit.*, p. 218
5 Orbach, *op. cit.*, p. 114
6 *Observer*, July 10, 1994
7 From the original manuscript of an article appearing in *Gender, Power & Relationships*, eds. C. Burck & B. Speed, Routledge, 1994
8 French, *op. cit.*, p. 203
9 Andrew Samuels (ed.), *The Father*, Free Associations Books, 1985, p. 3
10 Orbach, *op. cit.*, p. 106
11 Bettelheim, *op. cit.*, p. 196

Bibliography

The following volumes had a significant influence on my thinking about this book.

Althusser, Louis, *The Future Lasts a Long Time* (tr. Richard Veasey), Chatto and Windus, 1993

Baker Miller, Jean, *Toward a New Psychology of Women*, Pelican, 1986

Bataille, Georges, *My Mother* (tr. A. Wainhouse), Jonathan Cape, 1972

Bassof, Evelyn Silten, *Between Mothers and Sons*, Dutton, 1993

Benjamin, Jessica, *The Bonds of Love: Psychoanalysis, Feminism and the Problem of Domination*, Virago, 1990

Bly, Robert, *Iron John*, Element, 1990

Campbell, Anne, *Out of Control: Men, Women and Aggression,* Pandora, 1993

Canetti, Elias, *The Tongue Set Free*, 1977, André Deutsch

Canetti, Elias, *The Torch in My Ear*, 1989, André Deutsch

Chodorow, Nancy, *The Reproduction of Mothering: Psychoanalysis and the Sociology of Gender*, University of California Press, 1978

Coward, Rosalind, *Our Treacherous Hearts: Why Women Let Men Get Their Way*, Faber & Faber, 1992

Dinnerstein, Dorothy, *The Rocking of the Cradle and the Ruling of the World*, Women's Press, 1987

Eichenbaum, Luise & Orbach, Susie, *What Do Women Want?* Michael Joseph, 1983

Eichenbaum, Luise & Orbach, Susie, *Understanding Women*, Penguin, 1983

Hagan (ed.), Kay Leigh, *Women Respond to the Men's Movement: A Feminist Collection*, Pandora, 1992

Isay, Richard A., *Being Homosexual: Gay Men and Their Development*, Penguin, 1993

Jukes, Adam, *Why Men Hate Women*, Free Association Books, 1993

Kaplan, Louise J., *Female Perversions: The Temptations of Madame Bovary*, Pandora, 1991

Kitzinger, Sheila, *Ourselves as Mothers*, Doubleday, 1992

Lawrence, D. H., *Sons and Lovers*, Cambridge Edition, 1992

Hijuelos, Oscar, *The Mambo Kings Play Songs of Love*, Farrar, Straus, Giroux, 1989

Miedzian, Myriam, *Boys Will Be Boys: Breaking the Link Between Masculinity and Violence*, Virago, 1992

Miles, Rosalind, *Rites of Man*, Grafton, 1991

Mitchell, Stephen A., *Relational Concepts in Psychoanalysis: An Integration*, Harvard, 1990

Nicholson, John, *Men and Women: How Different Are They?*, OUP, 1984

Olivier, Christiane, *Jocasta's Children*, Routledge, 1989

Orbach, Susie, *What's Really Going On Here*, Virago, 1994

Phillips, Angela, *The Trouble with Boys: Parenting the Men of the Future*, Pandora, 1993

Piontelli, Alessandra, *From Fetus to Child: An Observational and Psychoanalytic Study*, Routledge, 1992

Rich, Adrienne, *Of Women Born, Motherhood as Experience and Institution*, Virago, 1986

Roberts, Yvonne, *Mad About Women: Can There Ever Be Fair Play Between The Sexes?*, Virago, 1992

Ruse, Michael, *Homosexuality: A Philosophical Inquiry*, Basil

Blackwell, 1988

Samuels, Andrew, (ed.), *The Father*, Free Associations Books, 1985

Samuels, Andrew, *The Political Psyche*, Routledge, 1993

Segal, Lynne, *Slow Motion: Changing Masculinities, Changing Men*, Virago, 1990

Stoller, Robert, *The Transsexual Experiment*, Hogarth, 1975

Stoller, Robert, *Perversion: The Erotic Form of Hatred*, Maresfield Reprints, 1986

Welldon, Estela V., *Mother, Madonna, Whore: The Idealization and Denigration of Motherhood*, Free Association Books, 1988

Index

235

FAMILY VALUES
A Lesbian Mother's Fight for Her Son

Phyllis Burke

When her lesbian partner gave birth through donor insemination, it seemed only natural that Phyllis Burke should adopt the child as its second legal mother. But as it became apparent that, even in liberal San Francisco, there were powerful forces ranged against her fight for recognition, Burke's perception of her lesbian identity was tested as never before.

Previously suspicious of the militancy of gay activist groups like Queer Nation, Burke now found herself increasingly drawn to their proactive stance as her entry into motherhood and love for her son sparked a growing radicalization.

Written with a novelist's eye, *Family Values* is Phyllis Burke's extraordinary account of motherhood in the face of ignorance and prejudice - a story of civil rights, political warfare, Hollywood, and scraping spaghetti off the floor.

'An eloquent response to right-wing groups ... which attempt to portray lesbians and gay men as being anti-family. The reader can only cheer.'
Los Angeles Times Book Review

'A blisteringly funny insider's look at identity politics, lesbian motherhood, and the cultural "image wars" that are becoming so central to national debate.'
Naomi Wolf, author of *The Beauty Myth*

Abacus
0 349 10638 X

THE NEW PRIMAL SCREAM

Dr Arthur Janov

When *The Primal Scream* was published in 1970 it caused
an international sensation. It introduced a revolutionary
new approach to psychological thinking, Primal Therapy,
which encourages patients to relive core experiences instead of
taking refuge from reality in the comfortable half-world of
neurosis. *The New Primal Scream* takes the theory even further,
showing that repressed pain is bad not only for mental but also
for physical health. Citing case histories, Dr Janov shows how
the application of his therapy has helped victims of incest and
other abuse overcome subsequent illness. The implications
are as devastating as the therapy is revealing.

Abacus
0 349 10203 1

THE MAN WHO TASTED SHAPES

Richard E. Cytowic M.D.

Imagine a world of salty visions, purple odours, square tastes and green wavy symphonies. Although only ten people in a million experience the world in this manner - the result of a condition called synesthesia that has baffled scientists for over two centuries - neurologist Richard Cytowic demonstrates that by understanding the workings of this peculiar state we can gain surprising insights into how all human minds function.

In 1979, Dr Cytowic met a man who literally tasted shapes. Soon after, he met a woman who heard and smelled colours. Here he tells the captivating stories of these individuals - and in doing so introduces us to the extraordinary potential of the human mind.

'Intriguing and entertaining'
Sunday Times

'Welcome and accessible ... Cytowic brings all the imagination of a novelist to bear on his exploration of synesthesia. Cytowic is fascinated and, after reading him, so are we'
Vogue

'Richard Cytowic is a revolutionary. He proposes an iconoclastic theory of how our brains are organised that has far-reaching implications for how we regard ourselves as human beings. This is an important book that everyone should - and can - read'
New Scientist

Abacus
0 349 10548 0

THE FLOCK

Joan Frances Casey
with Lynn Wilson

'Positively, intensely transfixing'
New York Times

For almost thirty years people called Joan Frances
Casey compulsive, a workaholic, an overachiever, too intense.
Nobody - least of all Joan Frances Casey herself - suspected
that she was housing a 'flock' of over two dozen disparate
personalities, all of them competing for attention, each unaware
of the others' existence, all contributing towards her near
destruction. After the mysterious collapse of her marriage
and an inexplicable flirtation with suicide, she consulted analyst
Lynn Wilson, who rapidly diagnosed Multiple Personality
Disorder (MPD) and began the years of demanding and totally
unorthodox therapy recounted in this book.

We - and the narrator herself - become spectators of
a dramatization of her own life as different characters emerge.
Brilliant scholar Josie, worldly art-lover Isis, flirtatious
party-girl Renee, tough-boy Rusty and five-year-old Missy are
just a few of the personalities coaxed into reemergence during
therapy to reveal their essential secrets; and ultimately to make
possible the extraordinary integration of the 'flock'.

Abacus
0 349 10451 4

☐ Family Values	Phyllis Burke	£6.99
☐ The Primal Scream	Arthur Janov	£8.99
☐ The New Primal Scream	Arthur Janov	£9.99
☐ The Man Who Tasted Shapes	Richard Cytowic	£6.99
☐ The Flock	Joan Frances Casey	£6.99

Abacus now offers an exciting range of quality titles by both established and new authors which can be ordered from the following address:

Little, Brown & Company (UK),
P.O. Box 11,
Falmouth,
Cornwall TR10 9EN.

Alternatively you may fax your order to the above address.
Fax No. 01326 317444.

Payments can be made as follows: cheque, postal order (payable to Little, Brown and Company) or by credit cards, Visa/Access. Do not send cash or currency. UK customers and B.F.P.O. please allow £1.00 for postage and packing for the first book, plus 50p for the second book, plus 30p for each additional book up to a maximum charge of £3.00 (7 books plus). Overseas customers including Ireland, please allow £2.00 for the first book plus £1.00 for the second book, plus 50p for each additional book.

NAME (Block Letters) _____

ADDRESS _____

_____

_____

☐ I enclose my remittance for £ _____
☐ I wish to pay by Access/Visa Card

Number ☐☐☐☐☐☐☐☐☐☐☐☐☐☐☐☐
Card Expiry Date _____